PRAISE FOR *One Story, One Song*

"Wagamese's prose addresses both sorrow and joy with a gratitude that can only be earned. *One Story, One Song* speaks of lessons learned, personal triumphs, and wonderment. These anecdotes glow like embers in a hearth, temporarily dispelling the chill of the world outside, placating with gentle warmth."—*Georgia Straight*

"*One Story, One Song* proves once again that Wagamese remains Canada's premier storyteller, especially when it comes to perception, credibility, wisdom and good old-fashioned common sense."—*Western Native News*

"Through his creative efforts, [Wagamese] heals past wounds and finds peace with his identity as an Ojibwa man, a former alcoholic and someone who has witnessed the range of human flaws and kindnesses."—*Winnipeg Free-Press*

"The short pieces in *One Story, One Song* remind us of human beings' place in the world: We are a part of it, not masters of it. And by sharing our stories we share ourselves. By listening to others' stories, we share their lives and perhaps gain connections. *One Story, One Song* is all about connections, something we all need."—*Globe & Mail*

RICHARD
WAGAMESE

ONE STORY,
ONE SONG

Douglas & McIntyre

Douglas and McIntyre (2013) Ltd.
PO Box 219
Madeira Park BC Canada VON 2HO
www.douglas-mcintyre.com

Cataloguing data available from Library and Archives Canada
ISBN 978-1-55365-506-0 (cloth)
ISBN 978-1-77162-080-2 (paper)
ISBN 978-1-55365-643-2 (ebook)

Editing by Barbara Pulling
Copy editing by Lara Kordic
Original jacket and text design by Jessica Sullivan
Printed and bound in Canada
Text printed on acid-free, 100% post-consumer paper

Canada Council   Conseil des ar
for the Arts   du Canada

BRITISH COLUMBIA
ARTS COUNCIL
An agency of the Province of British Columbia

Douglas and McIntyre acknowledges the support of the
Canada Council for the Arts, which last year invested $157
million to bring the arts to Canadians throughout the
country. We also gratefully acknowledge financial support
from the Government of Canada through the Canada Book
Fund and from the Province of British Columbia through the
BC Arts Council and the Book Publishing Tax Credit.

For Debra, the continuo
in the concerto of my life . . .

Contents

Acknowledgements

THIS BOOK COULD not have been written and, indeed, I would not be on the planet, if not for the loving support of my wife, Debra Powell. That's the straight truth of it. This book is as much hers as it is mine, and my life has been enriched and empowered immeasurably by virtue of her presence in it. Life is struggle, and my battles have been titanic. But she has stood there in love, compassion, understanding and faith and helped me to my feet whenever I have fallen. She is the great story and the great song of my life.

There are others—Ron and Jennifer Sainte-Marie, Nancy and Peter Mutrie, Tacey Ruffner, Ron and Wanda Tronson, Pam and Bob Lee, Tantoo Cardinal, Joseph Boyden, Lyn Mac-Beath, Tom Northcott, Janet Whitehead, Lee and June Emery, Irene and Jon Buckle, Dawne Taylor, Kent Simmonds and Doug Perry—who have all been there when I needed them. This one is for all of you, too.

Thanks to the editing prowess of Barbara Pulling; to the folks at Douglas & McIntyre; to Westwood Creative Artists, especially my agent, John Pearce; and to all the people at my speaking engagements and storytelling performances who graced me with their praise and their delight at the power of stories to entertain, enlighten and bring us all together. You have only increased my belief in the process.

Oh, and to Molly, the Story Dog, who got to hear all of these before they were written while we walked in the mountains behind our home, a scratch on the ear and a rub of the belly for showing me what unconditional love and complete joy in the moment are all about.

Introduction

HERE IN THE mountains, summer has dwindled slowly. Paul Lake sits placid and calm, like a quicksilver slip of dream. It wasn't long ago that boats were churning through that water and we could hear the shouts of water skiers and wakeboarders all the way up on our deck. Along the shore there are urgent calls from shorebirds. They feel the change coming, the advancing chill. Soon they'll take to the air and leave us, and there will be no more loon calls as the sun sets in wild flares of colour behind the reddish jut of Gibraltar Rock. It's always awesome, the silence the land fades into. It seems to me sometimes that seasons leave us in the way people do, never just gone, but degree by degree, fading like the smell on a loved one's favourite sweater, until the vanishing one day evolves into memory. Winter arrives far sooner than the first twirl of snow in late October. It comes with alterations to the hue of things, deeper shadow, faded colours, the thinner ragged cry of coyotes on the ridges and the rich, deep mystery of the land itself in the pitch and beautiful dark. As the season shifts, you can feel that mystery approaching. Winter has always been the slumbering time, the season of reflection, of rest, of preparation for another season of growth that is always promised, always fulfilled. For me, it means the Story Moons are coming. Legends, teaching tales and oral histories come alive around firelight and candle, and the great rolling voice of my people, sustained for thousands of generations, is heard again across the land.

We are all story. That's what my people say. From the moment we enter this physical reality to the moment we depart again as spirit, we are energy moving forward to the fullest possible expression of ourselves. All the intrepid spirits who come to this reality make that same journey. In this we are joined. We are one. We are, in the end, one story, one song, one spirit, one soul. This is what my people say.

I think about this as the dog and I walk the timber road up into the skirt of the back country. You can feel the land change when you step away from roads and buildings and noise. You become attuned to another rhythm. It's odd when it first happens. You stand there looking around expectantly, as if you'd heard a voice from the trees calling your name. The longer you hold to that moment, the more clarity you receive. It's not a physical voice you hear. It's a spiritual one. When you break the connection that binds you to money, time, obligations, expectations and concerns, the land enters you. It transports you. It takes you to a common human time in each of our cultural histories when the land was filled with magic and teachings. The land spoke to all of us then. It whispered. It told stories, and those who came to it most often learned to hear that voice through the closed skin of their eyes, the soles of their feet, the palms of their hands as they rested upon stone and tree and earth and water: the storytellers. They brought us the secrets of the world we call our home, taught us to invent, to create, to imagine the space around us. They are the ones who showed us that the

earth is alive, and we are joined to her by breath. The storytellers culled teachings from her mysteries. They discerned
the truth that the planet we live on is but one small part of
a greater, more marvellous creative energy that we are all
part of as well. When we touch the earth, we touch ourselves,
and the rhythms we discern are those of our own heartbeats,
sounding in the context of the whole. Belonging. The articu-
lation of who we are as a human family.

This is what I've rediscovered in the time that my wife,
Debra, and I have lived here. Our home sits between mountains overlooking Paul Lake, twenty-five kilometres outside Kamloops, British Columbia. Mere steps away from
our driveway the bush awaits, and the long upward slope
of the land becomes a rolling peak a few miles off. There
are fir, pine, birch and aspen amidst clutches of blackberry,
wild strawberry, juniper and staunch mountain grasses that
plunge suddenly into meadow. Getting out there has become
a special part of my days. Morning walks, evening meditations on the deck and time just standing out on our plot of
land make me feel properly framed. The longer we are here,
the stronger that relationship gets and the deeper the truth
sets within me: we are all spirit, all energy. That truth is
built into the teaching stories of my people. It is part and
parcel of ceremony, ritual and the principles that under-
lie those stories as their foundation. As with the land, the
longer you spend with stories and teachings the more they
become a part of you.

When we moved here, we knew it was right. The first time
we stood in the middle of this half acre, both of us could feel
it, hear it, sense it. We channelled our energies and desires
towards making it ours. We bought this place in the late
summer of 2005. For a time, we made the three-hour-plus

commute from Burnaby, just outside Vancouver, every other weekend. Eventually, we moved here full time. The land called us back. We know that for certain now.

We've worked hard to make this our home. We live in a rancher-style house with a deck and a garage that we have turned into an art studio and writing space. It isn't large or ostentatious. Our place is simple and rustic, and it will always be a cabin to me. There's an old wringer washer that's become a planter in the corner of the yard. A wagon wheel leans on a pine. We've painted our garden shed and woodshed the same red as the house, and we're content to let the yard stay the mountainside it is. We drive a rusted twenty-two-year-old Ford pickup truck named Hank. I own a chainsaw. Our water comes from a well. When night falls, we are enveloped in silence that fills us, shapes us and sustains us. The land infuses everything with calm, with truth, with meaning.

I am able to remember here. I remember how the teachings came to me during those years I lived in cities. I recall people. I return to circumstances and events that shaped me. But most importantly, when I walk out onto the land I remember that I am Ojibway. When I murmur a prayer at the shore of the lake in the soft, rolling syllables of that old language, I remember that I am a part of everything, that I belong, that my goal, according to the teachings of my people, is to learn to live a principled life. I remember that, like everything around me, I am part of a larger story.

In the end, we bear away exactly what we bore in: a soul, a spirit, a song. Creator asks us to work at discovering the fullest possible expression of ourselves. When we do that, when we embark on that most definitive of tasks, we become Creator's experience of life. Regardless of how we make the journey, we grant the idea of life back to its source: the infinite power of the universe. That is also what my people say. Our story becomes part of the great grand story of Creation.

For many years, I travelled unaware of this immense responsibility. Like so many of us, I was preoccupied with the chores of life, the to-and-fro routines of getting, having and becoming. It takes a concentrated spiritual focus to realize why we are here—to live out the best possible story of our time on this earth.

You can't do that when your focus is on material security. You can't do that when your desire is to have. You can do it only when you realize that we all carry a common wish, a common hope. Love expresses itself most fully in community. So does spirituality. What binds us together as a human family is our collective yearning to belong, and we need to share our stories to achieve that. Stories build bridges to undiscovered countries—each other. A very wise man once told me, "No one ever pulled up to heaven with a U-Haul." What matters is what we bear away within us: the story, the song of our living.

The stories and reflections in this book spring from our time at Paul Lake. They are presented in four sections, based on the principles our traditional teachers sought to impart: humility, trust, introspection and wisdom. Those four principles are the cardinal points on the Medicine Wheel, and they represent the essential qualities each person needs to cultivate to live a principled life. These stories were written in the pale light of morning in our little house overlooking the lake. They are about the people, events and circumstances that have shaped the man I've become at fifty-four. They are about the magic I've found in being a member of this human family. Kin. A part of the one story, the one song we all create together.

EAST

HUMILITY

THE OLD ONES say that humility is the foundation of everything. Nothing can exist without it. Humility is the ability to see yourself as an essential part of something larger. It is the act of living without grandiosity. Humility, in the Ojibway world, means "like the earth." The planet is the epitome of a humble being, with everything allowed the same opportunity to grow, to become. Without the spirit of humility there can be no unity, only discord. Humility lets us work together to achieve equality. Humility teaches that there are no greater or lesser beings or things. There is only the whole. There is only the great, grand clamour of our voices, our spirits, raised together in song.

Living with Bears

THE BEARS START coming down from the high ground in late summer, when the mountain-ash berries, rosehips, saskatoon berries, blackberries and wild raspberries are ripe and fat. We see them on the roadside or lumbering along the hillocks, and as the days pass they become a fixture in our yard. We don't find it troubling. When you reside in bear country, you make a soul compact to coexist with them. You learn to be watchful on your morning walks and to make sure your property isn't bear-attractive. You learn bear time. After all, this is their land. They were here first. If anyone respects that statement, it's an Indian.

When you're out in the wild—or what's left of the wild in the Western world—there is a palpable sense of the unseen. You get the feeling you're being watched from the trees. That can be eerie at first, but once you're used to it, it's rather comforting. This is the original condition of things. Long before our world became the technologically driven, noisy, over-populated place it is now, many beings found respite in wild places, and people felt a natural connection to the land.

We can opt for the convenience of machinery today, using quads and ATVs and dirt bikes to get us deep into the back country, but nothing connects you to the land as easily as walking. Hiking in the acute silence up here in the mountains, you always sense the possibility of bears. For me, that's magical. Walking on the land also keeps you alert to things you would ordinarily miss. You hear things you are usually too busy to register, experience yourself as a true part of nature. Alone in the wild, you become keenly aware of who and what you are.

So I'm not troubled by the presence of bears. What does trouble me, though, is news of bears losing their lives after run-ins with those who occupy their territory. Some people think of bears as garbage-raiding pests or as vile predators intent on snatching the cat, the dog or the children. I'm not afraid of bears, but I am respectful of them. At our place, we keep our garbage out of harm's way until it's dump day and we can dispose of it. We're careful with our barbecue. Bears are prowlers and foragers, and we need to understand that.

My people say that the bears are protectors. In our Ojibway clan system, the Bear Clan is responsible for security and law. As totems, bears symbolize strength, fortitude, justice and wisdom. When my people see a bear in the bush, they always stop and look at it before moving away. In the Ojibway world, a bear is a spirit being, a special teacher. I've learned over the years to hold them in the same regard.

This morning as I wrote, Molly the dog growled. I looked out to the end of our driveway and saw a juvenile male bear reared up on his hind legs chewing on leaves and berries. He was a marvellous specimen. His coat was thick and unmatted, and he had the beginnings of the rounded shape that comes from good feeding in preparation for the long hibernation to come. We watched him until he finally trotted through the yard, across the gravel road and off into the trees. He was one bear in a country of them. I knew he would find a place to hunker down as the morning traffic increased and the high August heat built up. In the cool of evening, he'd emerge again to forage in the berry bushes that surround us. That's just how it is.

Every day now, the oceans are becoming more acidic. Polar ice is melting. Droughts, floods, earthquakes and wildfires are increasingly commonplace. Bees are disappearing, and there are fewer salmon in the spawning grounds. These are only some of the rapid changes happening all around us. Just as our human lives are affected by these changes, so are the lives of the animals that share our planet.

Bears are a grounding tool for me. Whenever I see one, I am reminded that the old wisdom has something significant to impart about how I negotiate my way in the world. I belong to a web of life that needs all its parts to sustain itself. The ancient teachings are not a romantic throwback to a vanished lifestyle but a resonant reminder of our contemporary responsibilities.

Bears are protectors, my people say, and this presence reminds us that the natural world urgently needs our protection. That is the bear's particular gift to each of us.

Spirit Place

THERE'S A POINT in our morning walks up the mountain when Molly and I are out of reach of everything. The timber road winds up from the Paul Lake Road, disappearing eventually into the heart of the back country. We always stop at the same small creek, and I hunker down on my favourite log while Molly patrols. Once Molly is content and I feel rested, we cross the creek on footstones I installed during our first year here. After we've rounded the wide bend a hundred metres up, we climb through bush that's unbroken except for the evidence of free-range cattle and the scat of coyotes. We've never encountered another person.

Once we reach the alpine meadow, a half kilometre farther on, there is suddenly the feeling of the land. There are peaks all around us, and the pronounced jut of mountain terrain. Nothing moves. There is only the wind for company; Molly and I always stop to appreciate the mysterious push of its presence. The land is empty and full at the same time. It can be intimidating up there. You feel the silence in your bones, and you're alone in a way that is sharp and unforgettable.

My niece's husband and I once snowmobiled three portages back into the bush to ice-fish north of Pickle Lake,

Ontario. It was the dead of winter. The engines sounded harsh in the crisp air, and when we stopped to drink coffee the abrupt drop-off into silence was eerie. Every movement we made was amplified. My parka sleeve rustled loudly as I drank. We were at the back end of an old trapline, in real wilderness, and we had the feeling of being watched from the trees. The day was sunny and cloudless, casting the trees into deep shadows. The lake glistened so brightly that we had to squint to see, even through the tinted masks of our helmets. I felt very small.

By the time we reached the lake where we wanted to fish, it was noon. The wind had died down, and we settled into our camp chairs to wait for the pickerel to tug at our lines. The platter of the lake was ringed with bush, so our line of view ended at the ragged treetops. Above us was only sky. The sheer white stretch of snow around us was unbroken except for the twin tracks of our snowmobiles. Any idea of human accomplishment vanished.

My people say that the land's curious balance of fullness and emptiness is spiritual. Sitting out by that lake, I truly understood how powerful Creation is. All it would have taken to trap us there was a bad spark plug. No one can walk fifty kilometres out of the deep bush in the middle of winter. So my realization that the land held all the power was not theoretical. I'd become a speck, a dependent child. I was a being in need of grace, and in one sweeping moment I became a believer in all that is and all that will be. Gitchee Manitou—the Great Spirit.

We caught a load of fish, and we cleaned them so we could deliver them to elders and families on our return. Then we motored back. As we retraced our tracks, the engine noise shrill in our ears, it struck me how easy it is to forget the elemental teachings we receive in this life. Our dependency is immediately transferrable, as mine was to the feel of a throttle and the deep roar of a motor. Once I was safe in the seat of an Arctic Cat, the insight I'd gained was gone in an instant. The land whipped by, and with it the notions of emptiness and fullness. I was back to thinking of myself as an independent being, a man, reliant on technology to define me. I had to remind myself that what was real, what was permanent, was what I'd experienced out there beside the lake.

There is no word for wilderness in any Native language. There's no concept of the wild as something that needs controlling. In the Native world, there's no word for control, either. My people say that humility is the root of everything. To be in harmony with the world, you need to recognize where the power lies and to respect that. It's simple to do when you're miles away from anybody else, but just as simple to forget once you're back on familiar territory.

On my mountain walks with Molly in the mornings, I'd only have to twist my ankle or pull a leg muscle to discover where the real power lies. The land can kill, swiftly and without mercy. But it is a generous entity. The land gives us life, and feeling the power of it around me reduces us to our proper size. Every morning I'm forced to recognize my fragility and to acknowledge my actual place in the scheme of things. That reminds me to cherish what I have and to be thankful for all of it. Emptiness and fullness at the same time. In the land, and in me.

WYSIWYG

A WHILE BACK, I got interested in the economic possibilities of the Internet. I'd been busy building a network as a free-lance journalist, and I was drawn to the idea that I might be able to generate regular cash electronically. I visited a number of sites that claimed to show you how. The trick was that it would cost a bundle to get the information. There were also all kinds of sites devoted to get-rich-quick schemes, but none of them would allow me to use skills I already possessed.

Nonetheless, I was determined to set up my own enter-prise site. I read a few manuals and checked out similar sites, and when I felt ready I began to design a web page. Now, I'm no Internet genius. In fact, beyond possessing the basic com-puter skills, I'm not very swift at all. So I knew building a website that would function effectively and draw daily hits would be challenging.

Fortunately for me, I discovered a process called WYSIWYG. In website parlance, that means What You See Is What You Get. Rather than spend a huge amount of time learning com-plicated HTML code, you can use WYSIWYG templates to build your website pages. The process is quick, and as long as you have a plan things usually go along smoothly. At least they did for this neophyte web builder.

Well, I got a site built. Then, unfortunately, I discovered that as far as marketing strategy went, I was severely limited. I have never been much of a salesman anyway and the whole keyword, search-engine-optimizing, monetization thing was beyond me. There was nothing to do but retire the site. However, I'm happy I learned about WYSIWYG, since the concept turns out to be as useful in navigating the real world as it is in cyberspace.

We live between worlds, Deb and I. We often move in academic, literary, artistic and well-to-do circles. We're part of the diverse group that makes up our neighbours, and we also share a reality with the tenants who live in our rooming house. Deb invested in the place four years ago. It caters to the poor and marginalized, the mentally challenged and disenfranchised. We've learned a lot from all of these daily border crossings.

The rooming house sits on a quiet residential street in Kamloops. After much renovation and repair, it looks like an ordinary, though small, apartment building. It's no longer the visible nightmare it was when Deb bought it. And along with all the paint, the mortar, the new plumbing, the electrical work and the carpentry repairs, my wife brought another element into that building: heart. More clearly than I could, she saw beyond the dirt, grime, disrepair and hopelessness that permeated the building. She saw the potential for true community, and she set out to create it.

It was hard slogging. First, we worked to eliminate the active addicts. We knew, as former substance abusers ourselves, that you can't help anyone who is running drugs or booze through their system every day. There were people living there who just wanted peace and quiet, and it was our job to establish that for them. After many months and many difficult interactions, the drunks and other addicts were gone.

For most of those who remained, life was drudgery: empty days, welfare cheques, the dispiriting to and fro between agencies where the staff were the only people they got to know well. These were people whose stories rarely get told. They were, and are, victims of life's rampant unpredictability. They became our friends, and sometimes our inspiration.

Take Robin, for instance. Thirty years ago, Robin was a mechanic and builder. There wasn't a thing he couldn't do with tools, and fast production cars were his passion and his joy. He was tall and lean, strong and capable. Then a horrible accident left him disabled. He suffered a brain injury, and the surgeons who worked on him left an open hole in Robin's head just above his temple.

He could no longer work. He could barely walk. He spiralled downward until he became a welfare stat. He had lived in that rooming house, a pit of despair, for more than twenty years.

When we saw that open hole in Robin's head, we began to question the agencies. No one knew anything about Robin. He'd been allowed to just drop out of sight. So we bugged people. We bugged the brain injury people and the home care people and welfare workers and community-living advocates. Eventually we got some action. A year and a half and two operations later, Robin's head had been returned to its normal shape, and the hole had closed and healed. He walks better now. His eyes shine. He jokes with us and accepts regular visits from the other tenants who want to watch TV, especially the shows featuring production car racing.

Before we came along, Robin's room hadn't been painted or maintained in all the time he'd lived there. The former landlord just hadn't cared. Robin had one friend who visited him. He managed on the $500 that welfare provided monthly, though there wasn't much left after the landlord had taken out $375 for rent. Yet even after we got Robin the medical attention he deserved, he had no unkind words to say about anyone or about his situation. Instead, he took it all with grace, dignity and a measure of good humour. He still lives in the meagre, humble way he has to, and he always has a smile and a joke for us. What you see is what you get. That's how Robin is.

There are others in that rooming house with similar tales, people to whom life happened while they were looking the other way. Stewart, a former engineer whose mental decline led him to homelessness. Samantha, whose husband abandoned her and left her penniless when she developed multiple sclerosis. Jennifer, a former nurse. Tim, an athlete and contractor who could no longer work after suffering a brain aneurysm. They had all landed on the street, incredulous at finding themselves there.

None of these folks grouse about their circumstances, either. None of them blames anybody else. They just live their lives and behave like the people they are. What you see is what you get.

Deb and I meet many people in the moneyed world who try incredibly hard to be seen as important. Status is the ultimate qualifier. Keeping up with the Joneses is the great, grand chase, even when the Joneses don't give a damn about you. Their world is the HTML code of life-building: complicated, tricky, time-consuming, confusing and accessible only to the elite.

Our tenants don't confuse belongings with status. They don't confuse money with worth. They don't waste time on blame and denigration. They just live. When they talk to us, there's no decoding necessary. We know who they are, and we're comfortable in their company. What you see is what you get. From where I sit, they're the ones who've got it right.

On the Wings of Eagles

I'VE NEVER BEEN a graceful person, though I've always wanted to be. Ever since I first saw Gene Kelly dance on television, I've craved the gift of fluid motion. In the years since, I've watched Gregory Hines tap dance, Mikhail Baryshnikov leap, Karen Kain float. I would have settled for bending my body to the rhythm like the *Soul Train* kids did, but dance has remained a mystery for me. I can roll my rump and shake my hips to a rock beat, but that's more tribal excitement than real dancing. Deb and I attempted to learn ballroom dancing once, but it was a disaster. I was so busy trying to remember where my feet went that I was incapable of anything else. I couldn't keep my arms in position because I was concentrating so hard on counting out the time. It worked much better for us when she led and I settled for being pushed around in the right direction. As a young man, I came closest to being graceful on the baseball field. I could read the path of a ball off the bat from centre field, and my running catches were often spectacular. At shortstop, I could whirl and fire the ball across the infield like nobody's business. But when the cleats were off and the dancing shoes were on for the last night of weekend tournaments, I regressed to hopeless floundering.

One afternoon in the summer of 1989, my friend and elder Jack Kakakaway and I were walking through the foothills outside Calgary. It was medicine time, and we were scouting sweetgrass to gather for ceremony. There was never a lot of conversation between us when we were out on the land. Jack believed that moving in silence was the best way to hear the land speaking to you. So we were content just to walk and allow our senses to become attuned. As we topped a small rise, we watched an eagle soar across a wide expanse of bush. I felt honoured to witness the display of its strength and grace.

"That's how I've always wanted to be," I told Jack. "Graceful. Just like that."

He smiled at my words. We continued walking for a long time. Then Jack sat down on a log in a clearing and motioned for me to sit beside him. Those times were magical for me. Jack would talk openly about the land, share stories and teachings about how the plants around us were used and what they represented for our people. I was a rapt audience of one, and what he said to me that day has never left me.

"You only admire the display," he said. "The important thing is how the eagle learned to do that."

He explained that the eagle's grace doesn't come easily. The bird's flight looks effortless, but we miss the teaching if we see only the end product. Each eagle feather is made up of thousands of tiny filaments, Jack said, and the eagle has to control them all, whether the wind is blowing or the air is still. Only that skill will keep the eagle aloft. Just as importantly, the eagle must learn how to see the world, reading the treetops and the grasses for information.

There are no flying lessons. One day the young eaglets stand at the rim of their nest with the whole world in front of them. They can hear the call of their parents high above. To fulfill their destiny and become who they were created to be, each of them must make that first frightening jump, test their ability to fly. The lessons for us in the eagle's first leap concern courage and faith. All of us need courage and faith to soar.

Uncovering your gifts is a spiritual process. That's what an eagle in magnificent flight can remind us of. It isn't easy to be graceful. You must learn to really see the world and negotiate it, and that takes humility. Practising with courage will allow us to develop faith, the abiding knowledge that we are blessed.

Full of grace. Grace-full. Degree by degree, over the years, I've tried to practise the eagle's teaching in my life. I still can't dance, but I've learned that sometimes I can fly.

What We Share

THERE'S AN AIRY sort of confidence in knowing that you've seen your share of ups and downs. Staying on your feet, answering the bell for the next round, is what we mean by maturity. But for many years I found it difficult to see my life as anything but a series of injustices and slights. Being a Native person seemed a prescription for agony. I wrestled with a need to square the deal.

For a long time, my main motivation was payback. Every success, every forward step, was an opportunity for showmanship, for sneering in the face of society. I had a "look what I can do despite you" sort of swagger. Anger creates barriers. Resentment builds distance. But I didn't know that then. All I knew was that indifference relayed back to the source was what life asked of me, and I was hell-bent on delivering.

It made things difficult, that constant measuring up. Some good people are no longer in my life because of my relentless cultural and political one-upmanship. I broke hearts and relationships because I couldn't see any other way of easing the churning in my belly. Then I met Jack Kakakaway.

Jack was an Ojibway man who'd fought in a war, beat the bottle, found his cultural centre and reclaimed a ceremonial, traditional life for himself. He was a teacher, and a good one. I think he saw a lot of himself in me. He recognized the angst, the feeling of being lost that was masked as protest. Jack Kakakaway understood my heart and spirit far better than I did, and when he began to guide me I think that was his own form of payback, a thanks for the gift of grace in his life. He led me to ritual and the stories of my people. He helped me to see who I was and led me to a vision of who I might become.

Jack and I were talking one day about the challenges I saw to my burgeoning sense of identity. I spouted off about the Canadian mosaic and the displacement I felt as a First Nations person. I felt threatened by the new Multiculturalism Act. I believed it was an assimilationist document that would cause us to lose our identities and our rights as First Peoples.

Jack listened as he always did, with an expression I couldn't quite read and a half smile at the corner of his lips. Then he said something I'll never forget: "All tribal people are the same." He took his time answering when I asked him what he meant. Elders do that a lot. They force you to sit with your question, so that you understand there are no simple answers in matters of the soul. By making you wait, they help you to develop patience. They guide you to mindfulness and a sharpened ability to listen.

"There are no pure cultures any more," Jack said finally. He meant that everyone has to let go of something in order to get something else. As First Nations people, he said, we had to let go of snowshoes and toboggans to get snowmobiles and pickup trucks. We had let go of smoke signals to get telephones. Ultimately, we had let go of our languages to speak English. It was the same for everyone everywhere, he said. The world asks us to sacrifice something in order to be included.

What we need to look for in this world, Jack Kakakaway told me, are the things we share. There are as many things that make us the same as there are those that make us different. The difficulty is seeing them. The things that join us are as basic as breathing, as small as a tear. We all began as people huddled in a band around a fire in the night. We all longed for the comfort of a voice in the darkness. We've all sacrificed part of our identity to become a part of the whole. What we've lost is what binds us, what makes us the same.

Old Jack has been gone more than sixteen years now, but I've always remembered his teaching. It changed my life. I moved away from my us-and-them mentality and started looking for what makes people alike. That's what life really asks of us, and it's the most humble, yet profound, gift we can offer one another.

The Path to Healing

I AM A VICTIM of Canada's residential school system. I never attended a residential school, so I cannot say that I survived one. However, my parents and my extended family members did. The pain they endured became my pain, too.

At the time I was born, my family still followed the seasonal nomadic ways of traditional Ojibway people. In the rolling territories surrounding the Winnipeg River in northwestern Ontario, they fished, hunted and trapped. My first home was a canvas army tent hung from a spruce bough frame. Some of the first sounds I heard were the calls of the loon, the snap and crackle of a fire and the low, rolling undulations of Ojibway talk. My mother, my siblings and I lived communally with my matriarchal grandparents and some aunts, uncles and cousins.

But there was a spectre in our midst.

Having attended residential school, the members of my family returned to the land bearing heavy psychological, emotional and spiritual burdens. Despite my mother's staunch declarations in later life that she had learned good things there—she'd found Jesus and the gospel, learned how to keep a house—she was wounded in ways she could not voice. Each of the adults had suffered in an institution that tried to scrape the Indian out of their insides, and they came back to the bush raw, sore and aching. Their pain blinded them to the incredible healing powers within traditional Indian ways. And once they discovered that alcohol could numb their deep hurt and isolation, we ceased to be a family.

From within their trauma, the adults around me struck out vengefully, like frightened children. When I was a toddler, my left arm and shoulder were smashed. Left untreated, my arm hung backwards in its joint. Over time, it atrophied and withered. My siblings and I endured great tides of violence and abuse. We were beaten, nearly drowned and terrorized. We took to hiding in the bush and waiting until the shouting and cursing of the drunken adults had died away. Those long nights were cold and very frightening. In the dim light of dawn, the eldest of us would sneak back into camp to get food and blankets.

In the winter of 1958, when I was almost three, the adults left my two brothers, my sister and me alone in the bush camp across the bay from the tiny railroad town of Minaki. The wind was blowing bitterly, and our firewood ran out at the same time as our food. When it became apparent that we would freeze to death without wood, my older sister and brother hauled my younger brother and me across the frozen bay on a sled piled with furs. We huddled at the railroad depot, cold, hungry and crying. A passing Ontario provincial policeman found us and took us to the Children's Aid Society. I would not see my mother or my extended family again for twenty-one years.

I lived in two different foster homes until I was adopted at age nine. I left my adoptive home at age sixteen. For years after that, I lived on the street or in prison. I became a drug user and an alcoholic. I was haunted by fears and bad memories. Although I was too young to remember what had happened, I carried the residual trauma of my toddler years. I grew up ashamed and angry that there was no one to tell me who I was or where I had come from.

As a writer and a journalist, I have spoken to hundreds of residential school survivors. Their stories have told me a great deal about how my own family had suffered. At first, I ascribed all of my pain to the residential schools, and I hated those I held responsible. I blamed the churches that had run those schools for my alcoholism, my loneliness, my fears and my failures. In my mind, I envisaged a world where I could have grown up as a fully functioning Ojibway, and that glittered in comparison to the pain-wracked life I had lived. But finally, I'd had enough of the anger. I was tired of being drunk and full of blame. I was tired of fighting against something that could not be confronted. My life was slipping away on me, and I did not want to grow old still clinging to my fury.

After considering my situation, I decided that I would visit a church. I had had religion forced on me in my adopted home, and churches had run the residential schools that shredded the spirit of my family. If I were to lose my anger, I reasoned, I would need to face the root of it. I determined that I would take myself to a church, sit there and listen to the service. I chose a United church, because they had been the first group to issue an apology for their role in the residential school debacle. The United Church was the first to publicly declare responsibility for the hurt that had crippled generations and to make a tangible motion towards reconciliation. That put it in a more favourable light with me.

No one spoke to me as I took my seat in a pew near the back that first Sunday morning. There were no other Native people present, and when the service began I heard everything through the tough screen of rage. Then I noticed an old woman beside me sitting with her eyes closed. She looked calm and peaceful, and there was a glow to her features that I coveted. So I closed my eyes, too, tilted my head back and listened. What I heard then was the unassuming voice of the minister telling a story about helping a poor, drug-addicted woman on the street despite his own fear and doubt. What I heard was the voice of compassion.

I went back the next week. Again I listened to the minister with my eyes closed. This time he talked about some lessons he had learned while waiting in the grocery line and being stuck in freeway traffic. I was surprised. Here was a man responsible for directing the lives of his congregation, and he was talking about his own spiritual shortcomings. There was no self-aggrandizement, no implied superiority.

I went back to that church many times in the weeks that followed. The messages I got were about our search as humans for a sense of comfort and belonging. I don't know exactly when my rage and resentment disappeared. I only know there came a time when I could see that all of the messages were about healing, about love and kindness and trust and an abiding faith in a God, a Creator. There was nothing to be angry about in any of that.

After I came home to my people, I sought out teachers and healers and ceremonies. I committed myself to learning the spiritual principles that had allowed Native peoples to sustain themselves through incredible changes. I adopted many of those teachings in my daily life, and every ceremony I attended taught me more about the essence of our spiritual lives. I realized that what I had heard from that minister was no different from the root message in our own teachings.

It's been years now since I sat in that church, but I have not receded into the dark sea of rage or old hurts. There are genuine reasons to be angry. The damage caused by the residential schools to both the survivors and those like me who were victimized a generation or more later is real, and sometimes overwhelming. But healing can happen if you want it badly enough. Every spiritually enhancing experience demands a sacrifice of us. For me, the price of admission was a willingness to let that solid block of anger dissolve.

As the Truth and Reconciliation Commission makes its tour of the country, I hope it hears some stories from people who have fought through their resentment and hatred to gain a sense of peace. We need to hear stories of healing, not just relentless retellings of pain. Despite the horrors, it is possible to move forward and leave hurt behind. Our neighbours in this country need to hear about our capacity for forgiveness and for self-examination. That is how reconciliation will happen.

It's a big word, reconciliation. It requires truth and true humility, on both sides. As Aboriginal people, we have an incredible capacity for survival and endurance, as well as for forgiveness. In reconciling with ourselves, we find the ability to create harmony with others. That is where it has to start— in the fertile soil of our own hearts, minds and spirits.

The Caribou Teaching

MY PEOPLE SAY that animals are our greatest teachers. They believe that Creator asked the animals to introduce human beings to the world, to be our guides and show us how to move gently on the earth. The animals accepted this great responsibility, and we have thrived ever since because of their teachings. They are stalwart examples of principles like harmony and balance in action, and, as my people say, that is our purpose here as humans—to learn to live principled lives.

So it was disheartening to read about the shocking decline in the population of Arctic caribou. I have never had the pleasure of roaming the tundra, but I love the image of teeming hordes of caribou pouring across the land. For many of us, it's a national motif.

Scientists report that the number of cows on the calving grounds has fallen by 98 per cent over the last fourteen years. Only ninety-three cows were spotted near Baker Lake, Nunavut, in 2009. That was down from more than 5,500 for the Beverly herd in the same area in 1994. The birth rate for caribou is now one fifth its historical level. For the Beverly herd, which once numbered a quarter million, the situation spells doom.

Scientists have labelled the decline of the caribou as "mysterious," but that's just a handy euphemism for "don't bollocks our funding." There is no mystery to the impending demise of the caribou. "Progress" has doomed them to extinction, just as it did another Canadian symbol, the buffalo. Here in the mountains, logging and mineral exploration have decimated great numbers of assorted creatures. Similarly, industrial activity has destroyed the calving grounds of the caribou.

In addition to the Beverly herd, five of the eight main western Arctic caribou herds are in serious decline. That's tough news for the Dene, Metis and Inuit whose diet and culture depend on those animals. Then again, disappearing Aboriginal people is a symbol of Canada, too. When the land is needed for development, what's a species or a culture or two in the long view of things?

Trying to harness nature is a foolhardy business. As a species, we've resisted learning that, and the earth is rebelling. My people also say there will come a time when the animals turn their backs on humans. When that happens, we will feel a loneliness like no other, and the world will become a barren place. Recent signs across the globe support the accuracy of this teaching. Everywhere, animals are in danger of vanishing. Natural disasters are increasing in size and frequency, and vast alterations in the earth's rhythms are taking place. Heedless, we march along to the beat of progress. We allow industry to increase its carbon emissions or to police itself in meeting carbon limits that are ineffective in producing real results. Some scientists would have us believe that global warming is simply a fashionable theme rather than a phenomenon that threatens us with extinction. Meanwhile, the caribou are leaving us.

The spirit teaching of the great caribou herds is community. They offer us a model of interaction that we would do well to adopt. Their presence on the land is an ongoing gift. Their disappearance would create a moral, spiritual and ethical vacuum. We can't allow our arrogance to create such holes in our relationship with our living, breathing planet. Our home is a finite place, and the responsibility for living here with respect, humility and purpose rests with all of us. I fervently hope it isn't too late to say, borrowing from the great Neil Young, long may we run.

Harmony

ACCORDING TO THE teachings of my people, harmony is the most difficult thing to achieve in life. The Old Ones say that the pursuit of harmony is a lifelong endeavour. Because of the intense struggle along the way, the journey is a spiritual one. There are not many who choose to make it, and it's easy to see why.

To seek harmony is to seek truth, and truth seekers have always had a rough go of it in this world. Those who see life as something to be solved, put in order and contained are constantly bending truth to their own demands. But my people knew there was one thing that would never change. They knew there was an energy that brought all things together and held them there in balance. A Great Spirit. A great mystery. They honoured that mystery not by trying to explain it but simply by recognizing and celebrating it.

In the Aboriginal way of seeing the world, everything is alive. Everything exists in a never-ending state of relationship. If there is order to be found, it lies in the all-encompassing faith in this belief.

When the dog and I discovered deer carcasses strewn alongside the timber road where we walked, I was deeply distressed. Hunters had shot the deer and left their bodies behind. One pair, humped together under a sheet of plastic, had been beheaded. Creatures had been visiting the carcasses: coyotes, ravens, eagles, magpies, probably bobcats.

Over the week that followed, Molly and I came across half a dozen dead deer all left in the same condition. Their legs had been cut off and thrown into the trees. Near the creek, a head had been tossed in the grass minus its antlers. Up the road one morning, near a carcass, we saw a juvenile cougar slink off through the trees. The squawking of ravens told me of other bodies nearby.

The first emotion I felt was anger, bitter and churning. This senseless display exhibited disrespect at every level: for the animals, for the land, for the other people who used that road and for the planet itself. Empty coffee containers, beer cans, cigarette packages and bloody rope were strewn everywhere. The behaviour of these hunters had been careless, thoughtless and crude. I stomped off down the hill to warn my neighbours about the proximity of the young cougar.

The next emotion I experienced was shame. It's hard to be male when others of your gender mistake manliness for a can of Coors and a rifle. It's tough to be male when people shrug off such disrespectful behaviour as simply "boys being boys." It's shameful being a man when, for some men, wasting and discarding has replaced sharing. What these men had done offended my sense of propriety, dignity and rightness in every way.

Strangely enough, I also felt lonely. I go to the land for the experience of reconnection. I stand there and I feel I belong in a way I don't wholly comprehend. Once you have been fulfilled in this way, you see everything around you as valuable, necessary and irreplaceable. When a life is severed, the loss of that life force affects everything else. I didn't miss the deer; I missed the idea of them. I missed their spirit.

In the end, I mostly felt sad. I thought of the multitude of woes that confront us all around the world these days, the planet reeling from the effects of our indifference. Displays like the one I encountered with the deer are at the root of it all. This is why the earth suffers—because the majority of us have forgotten the idea of harmony or never learned it in the first place. We've forgotten that our responsibility is to take care of our home, and we've allowed dishonour to replace respect. Every bit of trash strewn in pristine places is proof of that. It saddened me that people can't recognize the larger impact of their actions, or often the effect of their inaction, either.

We are all energy, cause and effect at the same time. Those hunters found it too inconvenient to haul those deer out and deal with them respectfully. They found it too inconvenient to care. This apathy may be at the heart of the challenge we face as a species today. It is sometimes terribly inconvenient to act in an honourable way. So the earth suffers. Our home becomes sullied, and harmony is fractured at every turn.

We are one spirit, one song, and our world will be harmonious only when we make the time to care. For ourselves. For each other. For our home. You don't need to be a Native person to understand that—just human.

Getting to It

AUTUMN DESCENDS LIKE rain in the mountains. The light changes, taking on a quality like the dimming of a candle flame, mazy and opaque. The deer turn a brown that's almost grey. The bears retreat higher into the ridges. Many of the birds fly south, and there are fewer loon calls from the lake as darkness sets in. The stars shine bright in the night sky like chunks of ice.

A change of season is a marvellous thing. It's a thrill for each of the senses when these great shifts happen. Fading colours. The smell of wet foliage. The taste of frost in the air. The chill against the soles of your feet as you plod up the mountain trail. The honking of geese far above.

Deb and I have a new woodshed that I built with friends at the tail end of last summer. Even though it's just a lean-to with a roof, I drew up a plan and made careful measurements. I bought the supplies and did the prep work alone. Then Ron and Ed, the Ukrainian brothers from down the hill, arrived to lend a hand. The shed is sturdy, painted the same colour as the house. Filling it with the wood I'd cut was hard work, but I savoured every minute of it.

Outdoor labour is satisfying. You're taking care of things. It's a step back in time to those days when our seasonal needs extended beyond putting winter tires on our cars.

Living in the city doesn't offer you many chances to engage in that sort of work. I was a hunter-gatherer only on Seafood Day at Costco. My outdoor skills were limited to pooper-scooping on park trails. My sense of self was locked into the hustle and bustle of a cosmopolitan life, and the Indian in me, the tribal, cultural, one-with-the-land spiritualist, was buried under urban grit. The changing of the seasons was marked by new items in the sales bins at Walmart.

Here in the mountains, there's always something that needs doing to keep life on the rails. That has been a blessing for me. It's like being reawakened. I've tuned into the seasons of my own being and taken steps to ensure a safe passage. I've had to learn things I am still clumsy and inefficient at doing. I'm the Neolithic man discovering tools. I'm Oliver Douglas on *Green Acres*. I'm *Canada's Worst Handyman*. I'm *Survivor: Kamloops*. But adaptation is the hallmark of our species, and bit by bit I'm gaining the skills I need, albeit with some minor injuries, a bashed-up ego and plenty of cussing.

I'm learning how to prepare for change, and that's the biggest lesson. Caught up in our fast-paced lives, we forget how to stack and store, how to gather and save, how to build, replenish and plan. We lose touch with the rhythm of things. We forget that we live in the stream of Creation and that each of us is an indispensable part of it. We forget that we are all family, all kin. Once you step out where the wind can get at you, it doesn't take long for the reawakening to happen. That's the splendid thing. The earth is a healing entity, attuned to us and our needs. Somewhere there's a stretch of open ground for each of us. Somewhere there's a patch of green, a place of calm in our busyness. When we find it, we meld with the spirit of the natural world. I know, because it's happened to me.

The woodshed is filled now, and so is the woodbox that sits by the cabin door. From the moment the chill of winter sets in, we'll enjoy a good blaze and a warm home. Taking care of things is the very best work of all.

What It's Worth

DEB'S LIFE AND mine underwent a huge change late last year. It was one of those unexpected things that rocks you back on your heels. We didn't receive earth-shattering news or lose someone special. But a seven-year business relationship was terminated, and that meant a substantial hit to our income.

Deb and I are both self-employed. At least we were. Deb worked as a business consultant, handling the daily affairs of a psychiatrist's office in Vancouver. She did it remotely, using a computer program that allowed her to access the office computer from anywhere. She kept track of appointments and cancellations, paid bills and maintained inventory. The arrangement was inventive and successful.

Whenever we travelled to my speaking engagements, performances and workshops, Deb trundled along her computer, office ledgers and journals. She managed that office from Saskatoon, Christian Island, Regina, Winnipeg and, one memorable time, from the front seat of a rental car on a stretch of the Trans-Canada Highway. She was a dedicated, loyal worker. The doc's schedule was busy, and his practice was thriving. She spent long hours keeping his records straight, advising his patients over the phone and making sure everything stayed on an even keel.

And then, after seven years of doing the job, Deb was terminated by fax. The doc didn't call to thank her personally for her years of work. The message she got was sterile and bluntly worded. That was hard.

I earn my living as a writer. My books come out regularly, although there's generally at least a two-year gap between titles, and royalties on sales are paid twice a year. I freelance in radio and TV and write for newspapers and the occasional magazine and journal. But my money arrives in dribs and drabs, so we lost a lot when Deb lost that contract.

Luckily, my wife is a financial genius. Everything we do is budgeted for, and a significant part of every dollar that comes into our house is devoted to savings. Deb has made shrewd investments over time. Her ledgers are in awesome shape, too, so when her job ended, she knew precisely where we stood.

Our lifestyle is simple. We live rurally, with no need for trendy clothes, four lattes a day or toss-away shiny things we see in passing. We get our books from the library. We download movies. We eat simply but well, and last year, in a crush of conscience over my age and my waistline, I cut out soda pop. We chop our own wood and use the woodstove to heat the house in winter. We have workout equipment in the studio, and the land is a great place to stay fit with regular walks. I still buy CDs, because I'm a music freak, and we each pander a bit to our particular joys, but we've always kept our acquisitions to a reasonable cost. So even before the loss of income we were living a frugal, sensible life.

The tenants in our rooming house have also taught us a great deal about managing on very little. That's really helped us to keep things in perspective. The people who live there have forged a community out of their collective poverty. They share cigarettes, food and supplies. They check on each other if they haven't seen someone for a few days. It's an amazing thing to watch, and it offers a view of marginalized people most of us never get.

In 2008, Statistics Canada defined the poverty line (they like to use the term "Low Income Cut-offs") for a single person living in a major city as $21,666 before taxes. Because they exist on social service payments, all fourteen of our tenants live on an income almost $15,000 below that determinant. Take Lionel, for example. He suffers from a mental illness and is chronically unemployable. He's so incapacitated he hasn't managed to get a diagnosis. Disability status would qualify him for a higher payment, but Lionel wouldn't allow anyone to label him as disabled anyway. So he exists on the monthly welfare payments he receives from the B.C. government, currently $610 a month. After paying rent, Lionel lives on $205 a month. If you do the math, that means he lives on $2,460 a year. Even if he spends only $150 a month on groceries, less than what many of us spend in a week, he goes hungry a lot of the time.

Last year, we bought slow cookers for all of our tenants so they could fashion simple meals that would last a few days. Everybody has their own refrigerator, too. But there are some months when the welfare payments are five weeks apart, and when you walk into the house near the end of that long struggle, hunger hangs in the air. I never realized before that you could feel someone else's starvation. Deb and I bought cases of food from Costco during one long month and left them in the common room. The food was gone in minutes.

Most of our tenants walk to the Salvation Army once a week for bread and pastries. There's a St. Vincent de Paul kitchen not far away where they can get a hot breakfast, and a mission that serves suppers. There are people who say you can't starve in Canada, but I'd challenge any of them to try and live like our tenants do for one month. Starvation doesn't just mean not having food—starvation of the spirit is long, debilitating and lonely. Few people ever think about that.

But the people in our building survive with grace. They understand their limitations, and they live within them. They've learned to accept, with a grim sort of satisfaction, that as long as they have walls around them and a roof over top, they'll be okay. They know they will likely never move up from where they are, but they appreciate small mercies and unexpected boons.

So, sure, Deb and I lost a lucrative contract. Our monthly cash flow has decreased. Our ability to be frivolous has been curtailed. But we feel gratitude for what we have. We're thankful for our ability to be productive and creative. We're overjoyed that our home is exactly the place we want, and we can't abide being away from it for long. The true spirit of Canada doesn't emanate from the glass and steel edifices of Bay Street, the tumult of the TSX or grand neighbour-hoods full of huge houses. It doesn't come from big business, corporate enterprise or the chest-thumping grandiosity of big oil. No, the spirit of Canada resides in those who strug-gle every day to be here. It rests in the hearts of those for whom the poverty line is too high to even reach for, those who trundle home the day-old bread, comb the alleyways for bottles or limit the laundry to once a month to make their three changes of clothes last longer. That's where the spirit of Canada really shines—in the will of the people who survive despite the deck being stacked so dauntingly against them.

So Deb and I carry on. We love each other, and there isn't anything that can knock us off that foundation. Low on cash, rich in spirit. Our tenants have taught us that.

The Real Experts

IN THE WINTER of 1974, I lived for a month in a nativity scene. It was outside a church, set back from the sidewalk about nine metres. There was straw in there for extra bedding; the floodlights gave off warmth, and two plywood walls helped cut the wind. For me, it was salvation. I was broke and hungry, and everything I owned I carted about on my back. I was trying to avoid shelters, since it was easier to get robbed or beaten there than on the street. No one ever bothered me in the nativity scene. From the street, I must have looked like a lump of straw. I crept out every morning long before anyone else was around.

I felt a measure of comfort there surrounded by the wise men, the baby Jesus, his parents, the animals and the huge glittering star at the apex of the roof. Even though the biblical story meant little to me, lying in the midst of such a great promise to the world allowed me to believe that things would change. I prayed for that to happen, actually. Shivering in the cold, sleeping fitfully, I vowed to do whatever it took to get out of those circumstances.

I hit the streets every day, scanned the classifieds, joined a job bank, but it still took forever to find a job. It was tough to do so with no education and no appreciable skills. Finally, I landed a minimum wage job in a hide-tanning factory. I had to clean the hides when they arrived, which meant scraping flesh and removing hair and stretching the hides out to dry. It was stinky, foul, nasty work. Minimum wage in Ontario then was $2 an hour. It took me twelve weeks to save enough for rent and a damage deposit.

The only room I could afford was one of twelve in a three-storey rooming house. It was about the size of a jail cell, with a small window looking out over an alley. The floor buckled in the middle, and the only furnishings were a wooden chair, a bed, a lamp and a busted-up armchair. There was a one-burner hot plate and a small sink stained red with rust. The radiators clanked and groaned all night long. In the dark I would often hear something skittering across the floor. Still, it was a home, and I was grateful.

I spent many nights tossing and turning in that room, listening to drunken shouts and radios blaring tinny country music. I can still smell the urine, spilled wine and old cigarette smoke that permeated the halls. I lived on tuna, Kraft Dinner and day-old bread and pastries from the Salvation Army. I washed my few clothes in that rusty sink and spread them on the radiators to dry. Life was hard, but I had a roof over my head, and I had hope.

I thought about all of this recently, when I was asked to give the keynote address at a national conference on homelessness in Calgary. Of the more than six hundred delegates, the majority were academics: researchers, report writers, study instigators and journal editors. The only homeless people there were the street artists selling their work in the lobby. I was the only presenter who had ever lived on the street, which I found odd and unsettling. Instead of delegates hearing the genuine voices of the homeless, they attended workshops and seminars led by people who earned their livings courtesy of other people's misfortune.

I'm guessing none of those so-called experts knew how concrete smells when you're lying on it, or how it feels against your spine. Probably not one of them had ever experienced the sting of a morning frost on their faces or the incredible stiffness that seizes your joints when a winter wind blows over you all night long. Dozens of them were there all-expenses paid, with cash per diems in their pockets.

Every person deserves somewhere safe and comfortable to live. It struck me that homeless people and Native people have a lot in common—we've both had industries built up around us. Government departments, social agencies, social workers, police divisions, university departments, hospitals, media and the odd film crew all depend on us. If Native people or homeless people were to disappear, thousands of people would be out of work. But participants deemed the conference a success, and plans were begun for another.

Having been around Native issues for thirty years now, I've seen how often we've been researched, studied and Royal Commissioned. The end result of all that paperwork has been more paperwork. Only fairly recently, when Native people have begun speaking for ourselves have we gained any ground. It's a similar situation with the homeless. Folks are so busy concentrating on the *issue* that they forget about the people. Homeless people should have a voice in any developments that affect them. It's not enough to study, analyze, survey or count them. Homeless people need to tell their stories, and we need to listen to them. It isn't sufficient to treat the symptoms. We have to treat the disease, and we can only do that if we get to the bottom of what causes it.

During the month I slept in that nativity scene, I didn't hanker for a professorial voice to speak for me. I would have liked someone to hear *me*. I wanted someone to know how it felt to have only a burrow in the straw to call home. I needed someone to know what a desperate situation that was, how scary sometimes. To understand how hunger at 3:00 a.m. is different from hunger at noon. How it feels to wear the same clothes for weeks or to have to wear everything you own on your body at all times so no one will steal it from you. I wanted someone to know all that because I knew from my associations at the hostels, missions and soup kitchens that I wasn't the only one who suffered that way. The spiritual comfort of that nativity scene was memorable because it was so rare, so elusive, so fleeting.

Part of our strategy should be employing homeless people to help end homelessness. They're the real experts after all. They're the ones who know how it feels, and that experience is worth more than all the conjecture, supposition and research dollars in the world.

New Shoes

THERE ARE NIGHTS I can't sleep, even up here where only the yipping of coyotes disturbs the quiet. When I get up and gaze out the window, I can see the silver sheen of lake beneath the moon. The cabin creaks. The dog pads across the living room to rub her cold nose along my shin. I can see the shadowy darts and dips of bats as they hunt above the yard. A furtive house cat prowls the line where mountain grass nudges the cultivated space of lawn. On nights like this I read or write or sit in the rocking chair by the window to lull myself into sleepiness again. I'd rather be sleepless here than anywhere else in the world.

I haven't always had a haven like this. Once, when I was homeless and in the depths of alcoholism, I woke up without my shoes. They were lined winter shoes, and I'd bought them with the last of the money I had. I'd set them at the foot of my blankets when I lay down to sleep, and in the morning they were gone. It was November in Ontario. Sleet was falling, and the streets were wet and cold. I made my way to a St. Vincent de Paul store. It wasn't open that early, but when the man inside saw me standing in the doorway, shivering in my sock feet, he let me in right away. The warm air made me shiver even harder. The man made me a cup of coffee and offered me a blanket to wrap myself in. He fed me a sandwich and a bowl of soup, then led me down the aisles and made sure I found a pair of shoes that fit.

The man let me sit in the store until I had recovered my body warmth. We talked about hockey and some jobs he'd heard about that I could apply for. He was friendly, genuinely interested in me, and when I was ready to go he gave me five dollars and invited me to come back again for coffee and a chat. I left that store with a new warm jacket, dry clothes and a good sturdy pair of shoes. But I also left with a thankful heart and a feeling that I wanted to repay his kindness someday.

Eventually my life changed. I cobbled together some part-time work, and that led to a full-time gig in a warehouse. It wasn't long before I had a room and had pulled together a small pile of possessions. But I held on to those shoes. I wore them until the soles were thin and the heels canted severely to one side. Even when I could afford a better pair, I kept the old shoes on a mat by the door of my apartment, through several moves. Now and then I'd buff them up and wear them on a day I had errands to run. They were a symbol for me of how the world could be.

Many of the tenants in the rooming house Debra and I run are former street people. It's a struggle communicating with them sometimes. Most of the people who are there are so direly poor and neglected that they've forgotten what they deserve from life. Many have lost the ways of graciousness and gratitude. Their speech is stilted and often uttered in whispers. But hardship can happen to anyone. In these turbulent economic times, a lot of us are just a few bad decisions—or a few pieces of back luck—away from being there, too. Remembering that brings us closer as a human family.

Helping someone else can be as simple as opening a door. It can be as easy as listening in a genuine way. And that's the way we'll change the world—one person, one situation, one act of kindness at a time.

Birdman

THE BIRDS ARE on the move. These days, they are the first sound we hear upon awakening. By the lake they're flocked around the bushes and the saplings. There are dozens of species, and if you cast a keen eye you can see them flit and dart. They're migrants, called by an ancient urge to fly north again after the winter. Red-winged blackbirds. Grosbeaks. Flickers. Water birds.

My people say the birds are child spirits. We recognize their innocent, exuberant joy even though we sometimes forget how to sing ourselves. Birds reconnect us to the song within each of us. That's why we miss them so much when they leave us and celebrate their return. In the splash of late winter sunshine, they're gleeful. Standing in the chill air to watch them takes me beyond time, its rush and its burdens. Even the dog is drawn to their energy as she sits at my knee.

As a young man, I'd always taken birds for granted, never paused to observe them or consider that they might have something to teach me. Then, at a traditional winter gathering, I heard a story that changed my way of thinking.

In the Long Ago Time, before the time of the Human Beings, one winter grew especially harsh and deadly. The snows piled higher than they ever had, and Keewatin, the frigid north wind, blew long. The cold was so devastating that the sap in the trees froze, and their limbs swelled and exploded. Everywhere in the forest was the sound of popping trees. It was a haunting sound in the darkness.

A small chickadee who was nearly frozen hopped along on top of the snow until he came to the base of a small tamarack tree. The wind was gusting mightily. As the little chickadee huddled close to the trunk of the tree, he begged the tree to lower its branches to shelter him. At that time, all beings could speak to one another, and the world was filled with their lively chatter.

But the tamarack was young and proud. It revelled in its fine shape and refused to lower its branches. So the little chickadee gathered his strength and hopped on through the snow, clutching his wings about him to stave off the cold. Eventually, he came to an old pine tree and moved close to the trunk. The chickadee asked the same favour of this tree. Seeing his plight, the pine tree dropped its lower branches to shelter the small bird.

Creator watched the drama unfold. She asked the tamarack why it had refused to help the small bird. The tamarack replied that it did not see the need to surrender its beauty to shelter a bird who would likely die anyway. Then Creator asked the pine tree why it had decided to help the freezing chickadee. The pine tree replied that it had felt the bite of many frigid winds and knew how lonely and terrifying that could be.

As a sign of the pine tree's compassion, Creator allowed the pine to keep its drooped lower branches from then on. Creator allowed the tamarack to keep its magnificent shape, but because of the tree's vanity and selfishness it would henceforth lose its needles every fall. The tamarack would always face the winter naked and cold, as an indicator of its lack of mercy and compassion.

I was as haughty as the tamarack when I first heard that story. I'd just reconnected to my Native family and my culture, and there was a tough battle going on within me. I worried that all my years of displacement had disqualified me as an Indian, that I lacked the necessary soul to really belong. So I used vanity as a mask, dressing in a flashy Native style— fringed moosehide jackets with elaborate beadwork, turquoise rings, hide vests and moccasins. I ordered shirts sewn in Native designs and grew my hair so that I could braid and tie it in traditional fashion. I did everything I could to hide my terror and loneliness.

That story about the trees and the chickadee got me interested in birds, though. When I started to watch and listen to them, I discovered a calm I had never felt before. I read bird books and got some binoculars, and I visited birds wherever they were, in marshes and forests, meadows and semi-arid deserts. I could sit for hours enthralled by their vitality and cheer. In their songs, I heard celebration. In their behaviour, I saw harmony with their surroundings. Seed eaters, sap suckers, bark borers, fishers, insect divers and birds of prey shared the same sky. Each bird had its own important place in the scheme of things. Most importantly, the birds taught me that it's not elaborate feathers that make you beautiful. It's what you do and how you treat your fellow beings.

Scientists believe that birds are more ancient than dinosaurs. Flitting and hopping among the branches, gliding high above, they represent a wisdom gleaned through millennia. Pay attention to this world you've been given, they seem to say. Sing. Celebrate. That's what matters most.

SOUTH

TRUST

TRUST IS THE spiritual by-product of innocence. My people say that innocence is more than lack of knowledge and experience, it's learning to look at the world with wonder. When we do that, we live in a learning way. Trust, the ability to open yourself to teachings, is the gateway for each of us to becoming who we were created to be. All things bear teachings. Teachings are hidden in every leaf and rock. But only when we look at the world with wonder do the teachings reveal themselves, and trust is also the ability to put those teachings to work in our lives. Trust is, in fact, our first act of faith and our first step towards the principle of courage that will guide us.

With This Ring...

SPRING IS THE time to plan the year's projects. There's some exterior painting to be done, the garden to be put in. A pergola or a roofed porch, perhaps, to be added to the deck. This year, Deb and I have a new project, too: we've decided to get married.

Both of us have been married twice before. This time feels different, though. We've been together going on seven years now. We've had trials and tough periods. We've also supported each other through difficulties and practised forgiveness. Each of us feels our best self in the other's company. We want to celebrate that and order it with ceremony. So last week we went to town to shop for a ring.

I've never been what you would call a conventional man. My life has been marked by some dubious choices, and even some crazy ones. The people around me sometimes wondered if I had a few wires crossed. I drank too much too often. I floated when I should have been seeking stability. I always craved the sort of set-down life I saw on *The Waltons* or *Bonanza*. I just never thought I'd get it.

I learned early in my life not to have expectations. As a foster kid, you drift in and out of other people's homes without fanfare or farewells. I wandered through my life picking and choosing things at random for the most part. So picking out a ring felt big.

We didn't want anything extravagant. The ring we settled on wasn't a "rock." It was simple and elegant. But it exerted a power I hadn't expected. Once we'd bought it, songs touched a soft place in me that I hadn't known existed. Certain scenes in movies and TV shows got me all emotional. I looked up at the sky with a sense of wild expectation. And I smiled more. Even without the diamonds, that ring would be a marvellous object. Gold exudes the promise of riches beyond measure.

When I first saw that ring on Deb's hand, I felt raised up. It was as though everything I had done in my life had led me to that one shining moment. Life is a crucible. If we can make peace with our experiences, come to see ourselves as valuable and worthy, we gain the ability to set our lives on a different, more nurturing course. We find the truest expression of ourselves in the people we love.

Looking at that ring, I saw the awesome potential of two spirits joined by the strength of a symbol. This is a sacred journey we're on, and it's the travelling, not the destination, that will be most important. Trusting one another, standing together, we're ready to embark on this exciting new phase of our lives.

The Knuckle Curve

THE SUMMER AFTER Grade 7, my adopted family moved to St. Catharines, Ontario. I'd been happy on our rented farm in Bruce County, the happiest I'd ever be as a kid, and the city terrified me. I needed the land as an anchor, and the fields and woods I loved seemed very far away. I spent most of that summer pedalling around on my bike. It was lonely. The layout of the city was foreign to me. Whatever neighbourhood kids were around had their cliques already established. But I discovered Lake Ontario one sunny afternoon. After that, I went there often just to sit on the rocks and gaze at the wide expanse of water.

I didn't know how to fit in when school started. I'd come from a farming community where cool was lemonade on the back porch and hip was what Grandfather broke in a fall. Once again, as in the other schools I'd attended, I was the only Indian kid. I was odd. I felt awkward and ugly and stupid. Most of the kids just left me alone, and if it hadn't been for baseball, that might have been the whole story of that first school year in St. Catharines.

It was the fall of 1969, and the hapless New York Mets were making a run at the World Series. My team, the Boston

Red Sox, had finished third and were out of the contest early. Now the Mets were on their way to becoming the Miracle Mets, and the baseball world was in a frenzy.

I snuck my transistor radio into my classroom. I ran the earphone cord up through the inkwell hole in my desk, then leaned forward on my elbow, with one hand over my ear. I was listening to the game when I looked up and saw Gerry Haycox staring at me from across the aisle.

Gerry was a big baseball fan, too, and at recess I lent him the radio. After that, we shared the risk of getting caught. The one with the radio would smuggle notes to the other whenever someone scored or something big happened. We were both cheering for the Mets, and it was hard to contain our glee when they did well on a play.

The World Series was the catalyst for our friendship. While other kids moved on to football or soccer or the other games of autumn, Gerry and I spent hours after school honing our pitching skills in his backyard. We'd take turns squatting in the catcher's pose while the other hurled his best stuff. We worked on two kinds of fastball, the two-seamed "sinker" and the four-seamed "gas," and both of us threw a passable curveball.

But the pitch we were desperate to master was the exotic-sounding knuckle curve. We'd never seen one, but we'd heard a pitcher named Dave Stenhouse had thrown a knucklecurve for the old Washington Senators back in the early 1960s. Knuckleballs are gripped with the fingertips, and the ball is pushed towards the plate rather than being hurled. Their lack of spin makes knuckleballs unpredictable, and the knuckle curve sounded absolutely deadly to us.

What we imagined was a pitch that sailed and floated like a knuckleball but had a vicious break like a curveball. A knuckle curve isn't a knuckleball at all, actually; the pitcher just approximates the grip. But we didn't know that then. So, hour after hour, we'd try to throw the miracle ball.

We'd each toss fifty balls, then switch, following the system we'd devised. You'd throw the sinker first, then the gas, then the curve. When you were ready, you'd start sailing knuckleballs. We'd cheer when a ball floated in and then dropped or darted unpredictably. We'd both get anxious when whoever was pitching announced he was ready to attempt the knuckle curve.

Fall turned to winter, and we still threw. We practised with snowballs on the street and in the schoolyard, wearing thin gloves inside our mitts. Our arms got strong and our aim got accurate. We could generally put the ball where we wanted by then, but we never unlocked the secret of the knuckle curve. In all that concentrated passion, though, Gerry Haycox became my best friend. We fell together because of the magic of baseball, and in the pitch-perfect love of that game we came to love each other, too. Of course, we never used that word for it. At fourteen, you don't often throw words like that around.

The Haycox family welcomed me into their home. Every time I sat with them at supper and heard them laugh together, I wanted that for myself. My home life was a classic case of square peg, round hole. It's not the pounding in that process that hurts the most; it's the bits of you that get shaved away. I was scraped raw by fourteen, though I didn't know how to tell anyone that. My adopted family were staunch white Presbyterians. They led a regimented, no-nonsense, linear life that brooked no disorder. Punishment was swift and harsh, and the wounds I suffered went far beyond the scars on my buttocks. Many times I wanted to beg the Haycox family to take me in, to shelter me. But I just watched them love each other and basked vicariously in the glow.

Once we started high school, Gerry and I grew apart. He went to Lakeport and I went to Grantham, so we saw each other only on weekends and holidays. The loss was another in a long line of them in my young life, and I felt it keenly. My high school days were marked by a deep sense of inferiority and shame. I did a thousand outrageous things and got into big trouble at home. When it all got to be too much, I ran away.

I went on welfare and tried to find a job. Mostly, I lived on the street. One night, in a cold drizzle, I stood at the head of Gerry's driveway and looked at the lights of the living room. I heard laughter. I wanted to knock on his door and tell him what was going on. I wanted to trust him with my desperation and my loneliness. But, in the end, I just walked away.

I played baseball until I was fifty, for the sheer joy of it, but I never learned to throw a knuckle curve. When I catch a game on TV, I still pay strict attention to the pitcher, just in case he makes that miracle pitch. And sometimes, when the nights are long and the quiet is pervasive, I remember my friend Gerry Haycox.

The Word

WHEN I WAS growing up, the striking differences between Native people and mainstream Canadians were often remarked upon. During the 1960s and 1970s there were tremendous strides forward in Native life. We gained the right to vote, the freedom to gather in public and to practise our spirituality, the right to retain a lawyer. But every inch closer we got to authentic citizenship seemed to widen the gap between us and our neighbours. These days, it can seem sometimes that not much has changed. Conversations with so-called liberal thinkers, and I count numerous friends among them, almost always arrive at the "us and them" barricade. The barriers erected by the Indian Act, the reserve system, treaty rights, land claims and fiduciary wardship only buttress their arguments. Native people are different. We're separate. We're a problem to be solved.

In my day-to-day life, I seldom feel like a problem. I work hard at maintaining my property, staying above the water-line of debt and taxes and enjoying the fruits of my labours at the end of the day. Sounds awfully normal to me.

The truth is, the lives of Native and non-Native people are more alike than not. As an Ojibway man, I have been marginalized, analyzed, criticized, ostracized, legitimized, politicized, socialized, dehumanized, downsized and Super-sized. One day, I will be eulogized. What ordinary Canadian can't relate to that?

In my younger years, I was uneducated, untrained, unskilled and unemployed. In the time since, I've been displaced, disenfranchised, disinherited, disaffected, disappointed, disconsolate, disqualified, disrespected, disquieted, dishevelled, disingenuous, dishonest, disinterested and sometimes discombobulated.

Struggling with my identity, I've been misinterpreted, misfiled, misjudged, misunderstood and misguided. I've been misinformed, misdirected, mismatched, misstated and misused. Occasionally I've been mistrusted and misquoted. These days, I'm mostly misgoverned and misrepresented.

Like most Canadians, I have been overtaxed, overburdened, overextended, overdrawn, over the barrel and overwhelmed. By contrast, I've been underfunded, underappreciated, and under the gun. Like my neighbours I've tried to be low-key and low-maintenance, to stay low-cal, low-cholesterol, low-impact and low-risk. Most of us know what it's like to be low-income. Like many others, I'm an ex-athlete, an ex-smoker, an ex-drunk and an ex-husband.

As a Canadian, I've had to be ethnic, multicultural, nationalistic and culturally specific all at the same time. I've learned to be open-minded, politically correct, gender sensitive, globally conscious and self-aware. I've had to embrace the New Age as I approach my old age. I've gone from the Good Book to Facebook, from fireside chats to cyberchat, and from being offloaded to downloaded in one lifetime.

I can be Googled these days. I can be faxed, text-messaged, Twittered, Skyped and video-conferenced. I have a website, poor eyesight, the gift of hindsight and the occasional insight. I'm a multi-tasking, formerly metro-sexual, techno-geek with an iPod. I surf the net, play with the remote, rip DVDs, burn music and tear it up on weekends.

We can spend time deliberating on our differences. But in so many ways our lexicon is the same. Let's start talking to one another, using whatever it takes: metaphors and similes, tall tales and bad puns, honesty and tact. Let's use language to unite us, not divide us. It's really just as simple as that.

Trusting the Land

IT'S A HEADY feeling being alone in the bush, leaving everything that smacks of civilization behind. There's real power
out there, and it doesn't belong to you. There's nothing finer
than sitting on a log for hours and quietly feeling the land
around you.

I was twenty-four when I went into the bush for the first
time. Oh, I'd camped before, spent time hiking the back country, canoed into the wilderness. But I had never been out on
the land with nothing but what I could carry. I'd always followed the Boy Scout credo to be prepared, lugging lots of
stuff along with me for security: axes, ground sheets, lan-
terns, gas stoves, fishing tackle, snare wire, wax-dipped
matches, maps, rope, a compass, a space blanket, a hunting
knife and a marine horn for scaring off bears.

Being out on the land with only the absolute essentials
was daunting. But my friend Walter Charlie had convinced
me that I had to break my dependence on things. Walt was an
old bush man who'd been raised in an Ojibway trapping family. When he saw how ill at ease I was in the wilderness, how
ashamed to know so little about our people's traditional ways,
he invited me to spend a weekend out on the land with him.

When I got to Walt's place, he looked over the items I'd brought. Laughing a little, he sorted them into two piles. We left all of my usual implements in the car, and he stuffed the rest into a small rucksack. All that was in there was string, fish hooks, fishing line, a knife, a change of clothes and a blanket. That didn't seem like nearly enough to me for the country we were headed into, but Walt was carrying even less. It was cloudy and threatening rain. I felt trepidatious, but Walt whistled softly as he led the way.

We walked in about twenty-five kilometres. The land seemed to close off behind us, and I found the deep quiet unsettling. Walt was a strong walker, and I struggled to keep up. He rolled over the terrain with a bow-legged gait, while I kept my eyes glued to the rough ground. It was awesome country, though, and Walt stopped often to let me drink it in.

We settled on the shore of a small lake to make camp. Walt asked me to get a fire started, but once I'd gathered kindling he told me he wanted me to light the fire without matches. I laughed out loud.

"Everything you need is here," he said. "You just have to trust the land."

He led us on a search, and we came back to camp with a stick of dry birch, a palm-sized chunk of the same wood and a flattish length of maple. We scoured the shore line for cat-tails, and Walt showed me how to peel off their dried fibres. We gathered thin strips of cedar bark and enough birchbark to create a mat. Then he showed me how to fashion a bow from an arm-length sapling and a piece of twine and to carve a drill from the dry birch stick. The drill was bluntly pointed at one end when I was finished.

Carefully, Walt demonstrated the technique. He showed me how to string the bow and to place the birch wood drill into the palm-sized chunk. Then he taught me how to wrap the bow string around the drill stick. It was taut enough to hold it firm, but loose enough to roll along the drill and spin it when the bow was drawn back and forth. He set the point of the drill into the flat length of maple and began to saw the bow and turn the point of the drill until the friction had burnt a hole into the wood. Then, taking a knife, he cut a notch into the maple almost to the newly burned-in hole. He set the whole apparatus on the birchbark mat and went to serious work with the bow. He put his shoulder into the sawing; the drill spun hard, and it wasn't long before a fine powder gathered in the notch of maple. Soon there was a mound of it, and he tapped it together with the blade of the knife, blew on it until it glowed and set it in the nest of bark and cattail fibres. He had a flame in no time.

Walt blew out that flame and turned things over to me. I struggled to replicate what I'd watched him do. The drill was wet with my perspiration. Walt was patient. It took me half an hour, but I managed to light that kindling.

Later, as we sat around a blazing fire, Walt told me stories of bush life, how my people had survived in that landscape and built a strong and resilient culture. He told me stories about learning things from his grandfather when he was young. The training he'd gone through had lasted years.

"Everything you need is here," he said again. "You just have to trust the land."

Walt and I went out on the land together a few times after that. He passed away when I was thirty. Though it's been years since I used a bow and drill, I've never forgotten the time I spent with him or the central message of his teaching. It's not the huge things that return us to who we are, it's the magic of the small. Sitting out alone on the land, I remember.

A Crow Story

THERE ARE CROWS everywhere around our mountain home. I like to hear them cackling and cawing when I'm walking through the bush, and they can get quite resentful if the dog's bounding through the trees disturbs them in their foraging. Crows are good companions on a hike. Their sound is ancient, and they lend a mystic feel to your time out on the land. They've been here a long time, and the example they offer us of a steward relationship to the earth is tremendous.

Crows are a planetary mainstay. I depend on their voices when I'm in the back country. Even when new snow densely coats the trees, and seeing anything is difficult, the crows can be heard nattering back and forth. I've always liked them.

In the Long Ago Time, when Creator sent Human Beings to inhabit the earth, she gave gifts to all the flyers of the world. The Eagle was chosen as the people's messenger, to carry their prayers and thanks to Creator. The Loon was made the teacher of love and good relationships, the Owl the possessor of patience and observation. The Chickadees exemplified persistence and harmony. But Crow felt he'd been given nothing.

He didn't have colourful feathers. He didn't have a beautiful song. He wasn't known for his strength or vision. None of the Animal People looked to him for special help or insight. Crow wondered what his role was in the circle of being. Every other creature seemed to have one. So he began to fly about looking for purpose. He flew far and wide, searching the world for one teaching that might become his own to carry.

Crow visited with Mukwa, the Bear, and asked for some of Mukwa's teachings. But Crow was impatient, and when none of Mukwa's gifts seemed to fit, he flew off again. For a time, he lived with Moozo, the Moose, and with Pizheu, the Lynx. He flew into the depths of the great northern woods to sit with Wolverine. One by one, he visited Wolf, Coyote, Beaver, Loon, Fish, Turtle and even the great Eagle himself.

Crow learned a lot on his travels, but he couldn't find anything that felt like his very own. The humility and devotion of his fellow creatures made him hungrier than ever for some special teaching he could offer. Then, one day, as he flew by a hollow tree, he noticed Squirrel looking sadly out from a hole in the trunk.

Crow landed and gently coaxed Squirrel to talk. Lightning had struck the tree that had held her nest, and she had lost her babies, she told him. Crow nodded with understanding. Then he took Squirrel to see the Bear and the Turtle to receive their medicine.

After that, as he flew about, Crow encountered other creatures in need. Each time, he stopped, listened to their stories and then took them to the animal whose medicine was right for them. He became a respected listener and guide.

Crow was never graced with a gorgeous coat of feathers for his troubles. He was never endowed with a beautiful song. His grating call perturbed the Human Beings, but the Animal People always felt more secure when they heard Crow croaking in the forest. Crow's gift, and his purpose, became the ability to communicate and to carry teachings and other medicines to help people.

When I heard the story of Crow, I thought it was simply a wonderful folk tale. I was young and in a hurry then, dazzled by bright and shiny things. Reflection was just what I saw in the mirror every morning. But the power of teachings is their ability to simmer beneath the surface. Now that I've reached middle age, I understand that Crow's story is about working with others in the spirit of friendship and service. When we do that, we find our own sense of purpose. You only have to hear a crow cawing to be reminded of that.

Honouring the Story

ISOTROPIC IS A thousand-dollar word that refers to something being identical in every direction. Astronomers invented the term. In the starkness of space, there is no up or down, east or west. Everything is stars, darkness and the whirl of cosmic activity. It's a directionless void, savage in its eternal beauty. Here on the frozen platter of the lake, with the mountains hulked up around me, I get a sense of that. Spring's coming, and the dog and I have ventured out while the ice still holds, to see it all from the middle. White. Unbroken. The sky above us is grey, tufted with cloud. Turning, with my arms spread out and my head thrown back, the world is the same in all directions. It's a heady and unsettling feeling.

A life can be isotropic, too. We've discovered that, Deb and I, in the years since she bought the rooming house. There's room for fourteen people to live there, and we've seen many folks come and go, most of them unable to adapt to a routine, predictable life. A parade of the invisible.

Before Deb invested in the place, the rooming house had been allowed to decay. The structure was sound enough, but the building had atrophied from a decided lack of care. There was a glumness to it, a sad ambience that spoke of lives left to decompose. The yard was full of broken bicycles, discarded shopping carts, old clothing and glass from broken windows.

Deb was shocked when she saw the inside of the building for the first time. People were living in Third World conditions. Some had nothing to cook on; their stoves had fallen into disrepair, along with their small refrigerators. The place hadn't been painted in decades, and the thick yellow layer of nicotine cast everything in a hazy kind of light. The floors were filthy, and the bare concrete floor of the central hallway was thick with mould and mud. Some of the tenants were drug addicts. Without any custodial management, they'd grown used to treating their homes as disrespectfully as they did their bodies. Garbage was strewn everywhere, and the front and back doors of the house were left open every night. The place had become a flophouse. People regularly crawled in and out of the first-floor windows, and the address was a regular stop for ambulances and the police.

Some tenants were wrestling with mental health issues. In their obfuscated world, these living conditions were par for the course. They'd grown so used to not having a voice that the idea of complaining, pressing for even the most basic things, was foreign to them. Their battle was for daily survival. They'd been cast adrift by the agencies and institutions that might have helped them. If they were on medication, there was no one around to ensure they actually took it.

Even though I had spent parts of my life on the street, in dire poverty and under the lash of horrific substance abuse, this situation appalled me. I worried that the project was too daunting, too big, might be too draining. But Debra is an amazingly resolute and compassionate person. She set to work to change things: to provide essential services, to clean the place up, to renovate it and to offer her tenants a human presence in the wasteland of their existence.

When she first started showing up there, everybody kept their doors shut like sad, hermetic shutaways. Since it was December when Debra bought the place, she offered everybody a big Christmas dinner that first month. She stuck invitations under everyone's door and prepared Santa bags for each person. The tenants who did show up for the meal ate quickly, silently for the most part, then retreated back to the safety of their rooms. None of them was comfortable being in company, having their back to an open room, having someone care about them. But gradually, as rooms were cleared of the violent and the actively addicted, as cleanliness and order became the rule, people's doors opened.

We worked hard at cleaning the place up. We washed walls and painted, scrubbed floors and hung curtains, fixed stoves and plumbing, carpeted hallways and secured the outside doors. Deb screened prospective tenants carefully, looking for people who wanted a way out of their harsh lives. She enforced strict rules of behaviour and decorum and brooked no breaches. Word soon got around that the rooming house was now a lousy place to drink or fix.

But the most important thing she brought to her house was humanity.

No one had spoken to these people in a meaningful way for a long time. They'd grown used to remaining mute, shrugging their shoulders in silent surrender. Debra took the time to sit with them in their rooms and listen to what they had to say, no matter how garbled or outright loony it may have been. She really looked at them. She saw those people, and they responded as best they could. There was no miraculous transformation. People continued to get drunk, to fight with each other, to isolate themselves. Some had to be evicted. But over time the house settled. The first year, eighty people came and went in those fourteen rooms. We saw hope flare briefly in some and then die just as quickly, when their desire for change was overpowered by hurt and drugs and booze. But a handful reached out for what we offered. They began to embrace rules and order, to care about a place they could call home, many for the first time. They started to care about themselves.

We've learned a lot from this experience. Life can pulverize your spirit. Personal pain, private horrors and agonies manifest themselves in the problems we shake our heads at when we see them from the safety of our cars. The concrete of the street cements in the soul, and it takes time and mercy to reverse the process.

Hopelessness is isotropic: the view in every direction is the same. That's the nut of it. It's hard to change when everything you see looks identical. It's hard to expect more from the world when expectation is the most painful feeling of all. It's hard to learn to trust when you've had to shoulder the weight alone for years and years. But healing happens. We've seen it. People stuck on the street are more than statistics or shaded areas of a pie chart. Their spirits ache for the same things ours do, in the comfort and security of our sometimes splendid homes. If we really listened to them, we'd learn that.

My people say that each of us is a story, part of the great, grand tale of humanity. In the end, the story of our time here is all we have. When you offer a tale in the Ojibway manner, you do so for the story's sake. If we could honour each voice in that way and allow it to resonate, what a wonderful clamour that would be.

Beyond the Page

I DEPENDED ON research to help me understand the world when I was growing up. During my late teens and early twenties, I practically lived in libraries. Whenever the grit of my days got to be too much, I found peace in the stacks, where there was material to help quench my raging thirst for knowledge.

I was ashamed of many aspects of my life in those days. I was a high school dropout, I had few practical skills and I knew next to nothing about who I was as a cultural or tribal person. Libraries offered me both escape from my feelings of inadequacy and entry into realms I never knew existed. I learned to interpret the world through what I read. Back then, it was achingly difficult for me to talk to other people, and books were my haven.

I'm thankful for all those libraries. The books I devoured made me employable. They let me build the enormous frame of reference that enabled me to become a writer. They helped me to discover the larger world that life and circumstance had deprived me of.

But book learning can take you only so far. Eventually, you need to step beyond the pages. That was illuminated for me again after Deb and I started running the rooming house. Even though I've been on the streets myself and have first-hand knowledge of what a struggle it can be just to survive, I quickly found out I was no expert. I've read sociological tomes, textbooks and research papers on poverty. I've audited university lectures on the subject. But when I came face to face with the people who inhabit the streets and alleyways and missions of Kamloops, I found I still had lots to learn.

Take a lady I'll call Shirley.

The agency that sent Shirley to the rooming house told us that she had a mental illness. They said she could be difficult. But they didn't share her diagnosis with us or give us a picture of what we could expect. They seemed to believe, as many agencies do, that the mere knowledge Shirley was incapacitated would enable us to provide secure, predictable shelter for her. But that wasn't enough.

At first, Shirley was quiet. She took her time moving in and getting acclimatized to the rules and the sense of order we work hard at maintaining in the house. Gradually, she stepped out from behind her own door and began to interact with the other residents. That's when things got difficult. As long as she was insulated, stayed private, Shirley could be fine. But when she stepped into the community, things got weird.

She phoned Deb and me at all hours of the day and night to tell us who was doing what and how disruptive it was to her sense of security. She complained harshly about the actions of other people. She yelled and screamed. She ranted. When we went over to our house to talk to her, she was usually bitterly angry. Sometimes she refused to open her door to discuss the situation. Instead, she screamed at people and insisted that we evict them, have them arrested and jailed.

Shirley's anger was toxic. Even when she was sullenly silent, her cold rage was palpable. Often, the events that had precipitated such vitriol were insignificant. Some had not happened at all. It seemed to us that Shirley sought out reasons to rant. We wondered both why that was and how we could help her. As the months went by and the explosions continued, we considered the possibility of having to evict Shirley for the sake of the other tenants.

Then, one day, she confided in Deb. Shirley is an Aboriginal woman in her late fifties. She's a grandmother. One of her sons had died from ingesting bad cocaine, and it was her overwhelming, inconsolable grief that allowed a crack to appear in the wall she'd built around herself. My wife went into Shirley's room and sat on the edge of her bed, holding Shirley's hand, comforting and calming her. Shirley told Deb that many years earlier, when she was seven months' pregnant, she'd been viciously assaulted and raped by three members of her family.

The story that came out of Shirley that day changed everything for us. We were horrified by what had happened to her, and after that, when we looked at her, we saw a totally different person. Shirley raged because she had to. Any slight allowed her to open the valve just a little and let out some of that stoked resentment, pain, fear and sense of betrayal. That anger was her only outlet. She'd never had a chance to heal. Most professional people had just tagged her as mentally ill and done nothing to help her find peace.

Now, when Shirley ranted and raged, we knew where it came from, and we sought ways to bring her long-lasting peace and calm rather than merely pacifying her in the moment.

Shirley eventually moved on, and she took her rage with her. She was too proud to face what she perceived as the indignities of therapy or professional help. The street had made her that way. When you're out there, people apply tags to you all the time. You're an addict, a drunk, crazy, violent, lazy, stupid, difficult, chronic, hard to house or beyond help. After a while, you start to refuse all of the labels, even if some of them might mean getting help.

Textbooks, degrees, work experience, shared life experience and even compassion can't give you someone's whole story. Only listening—reaching out from one human heart to another—can help you understand why someone is marginalized, impoverished, traumatized, wounded, addicted, drunk, isolated or chronically homeless. We are all created equal, and only circumstance and history make us what we appear to be on the outside.

My life would not have evolved the way it did without the world of books. Without this book knowledge, I could not have become the man I am today. But you also need to step outside the stacks and make contact with those who inhabit the world.

We all have stories within us. Sometimes we hold them gingerly, sometimes desperately, sometimes as gently as an infant. It is only by sharing our stories, by being strong enough to take a risk—both in the telling and in the asking— that we make it possible to know, recognize and understand each other. No book will ever be a substitute for that.

The Kid

WHEN THE MORNING sun breaks over the mountain, the light seems to magnify everything. From where I stand on a rock at the edge of the lake, the trees on the flank of the far peak seem close enough to touch. The reeds fifty metres out are thick with birds, and the clarity of the air allows me to see every detail. Beside me, the dog is also transfixed by the wonder of the planet. Every day, rain or snow or shine, we're out here in the early hours. The land, my people say, is a feeling—and that feeling is peace.

When I was younger I rarely felt peace. Since then, I've had the opportunity to heal, to reclaim the lost parts of myself, to reconnect to my tribal life. But on this brilliant morning, I'm thinking about a boy I met yesterday. He's fourteen. A white kid, tall and skinny. The man he'll become is evident in the stretch of him. He was languid and loose, like kids his age are, but there was a cautionary edge to him that spoke to me.

The boy sat on the edge of his chair, leaning forward some, keenly watching the adults in the room. His eyes flicked back and forth as Deb and I spoke with his dad. I could see the muscles twitch in his thigh, see him bouncing up and down on the balls of his feet. I could feel his readiness to bolt if the signs of danger came. When the conversation turned to talk of safety and security, I could almost hear him relax.

There was nothing in this kid that would declare him as radical or different: no tattoos, no gang apparel, no posturing, no piercings. He was dressed like any other boy his age, though a tad more shabbily than some, perhaps. It took closer inspection to see that he was someone who'd learned the delicate art of becoming invisible, of shrinking into the background and waiting, patient as a wolf cub, to see whether violence or peace would reign.

The boy's dad is a drunk. When Debra and I met him, he was coming from a recovery program he'd left early in order to pick up the pieces of his family life. It wasn't the man's first bash at recovery. He wore that evidence on his face. He and the boy were camped out in a low-end hotel until they could find suitable housing. They'd come to us to scope out a room in our rooming house. As the talk progressed, the man painted himself as a concerned father eager to provide for his kid. But I could see the street on him as he answered our questions.

It wasn't so long ago that I wore the same look. It wasn't so long ago that I roamed about looking for a peg to hang my life on, somewhere to get past the ache that booze leaves in your gut and your spirit. Street drunks and closet drinkers recognize one another when they meet. That's how you survive out there. You find someone who's the same kind of drinker you are, or preferably anyone who's worse off. That's also how you heal when you finally quit. You find someone who drank the same way you did and walk beside that person in sobriety.

The boy had seen everything. You could tell that. The fragments of his story we got in that brief time were about being plucked from his life and plunked down with strangers. About never feeling at home, wherever he landed. About not knowing from one day to the next when a sweeping change was going to come, when a blow or wounding words would hurtle towards him out of the darkness. About this stranger who was his father, and what it would be like to live with him functionally sober. The boy spoke quietly when he answered our questions. His voice was low and even, and the only feeling it betrayed was resignation. His eyes, when they lifted momentarily from the floor, were distant and devoid of hope. It made me want to cry.

We made plans for the two of them to take a room that would be available in a month's time. Deb and I decided to offer the room because of the boy. Both of us felt ourselves reach out to him. Both of us felt his pain. He wanted his future to represent something more than it had up to that point.

When I was fourteen, my life was bombarded by pain and isolation. I was trapped and alone, and I had no one to tell about it. I felt all of this in that boy, and it called to me. It's our brokenness that allows us to recognize and heal each other, not the fronts of stoic capability we display.

So the boy will come to stay. We made that happen, and we feel good about it. He'll have a place now to set his feet down, a place to rest. He'll have a home. It won't be perfect, but it's a beginning, a fresh start, and roots have taken hold in thinner soil. When the conversation was over and we stood to shake hands, the boy offered his. It was birdlike and small. When he looked at me, I could see the question in his eyes: will it be any different this time? It made me want to cry.

Sometimes it doesn't take much to change a life. My people's teachings speak of respect, the ability to honour all of Creation, and we honour it best through our allegiance to each other. We give what we can and stand beside people when they need it. That's how it works. Peace.

Gathering

HERE IN THE mountains, the dawn hours seem to stretch forever. The sun breaks elegantly over the top of the peak behind us, so that light appears to slide over the world. You can almost feel the shadows ease. The essence of the land is palpable when you step out onto it. It fills you. When the dog and I venture out at this time of day, we are silenced by the majesty of it all. Our walks are punctuated only by the call of the birds, the nattering of squirrels and the sound of the breeze. Animal talk. My people say that in the beginning, the animals could speak with each other, and there's still a sense of those ancient times, like a whispered conversation. The Indian in me is drawn to it. I stand on a rock above the water, close my eyes and pull the feeling into me with each breath. Indian. Ojibway. Human.

Deb and I gathered with friends recently. Our hosts were Ed and Arlene, former Edmontonians who moved here after Ed's insurance career had run its course. If being retired means a devoted tending to house and home, then that's what Ed and Arlene are. Ed and his brother Ron married two sisters. Arlene and Carol are fastidious and loyal, Catholic in their upbringing. Their lakefront homes are immaculate and charming. The two families live two houses apart, and there's a well-worn path between their doors. They are linked by a blood that's thicker than most, and there's a tightness to their connection that you can feel. At this gathering, there were brothers, sons, daughters, cousins and grandkids.

The adults convened in the living room, looking out onto the lake. The kids disappeared to the basement rec room, where they watched videos and occasionally meandered up to peek at us and cadge cookies or juice. A fat, well-tended cat prowled the room. A newborn baby girl, Ed and Arlene's granddaughter, Olivia, lay in her aunt's arms, staring wide-eyed at everything. It was comforting to sit in the influence of their togetherness. We talked about everything from plumbing to well water, woodpiles to cougars spotted on the road, gas prices, vacations, home renovations and hockey. We've known these folks for less than two years, but we are comfortable enough with each other to tease and joke and banter. The talk had a life of its own, and we followed the energy wherever it took us.

Ed and Ron are from Ukrainian farmer stock, and Arlene had prepared a sumptuous spread of ethnic foods for the event. Thankfully, we Ojibways are omnivores, and I dug in heartily. Even if I avoided the head cheese, I lost myself in the plenty. Arlene and Carol hovered over everything, gently badgering us to eat more before they sat down to enjoy the meal.

After supper, the guitars came out, and three of us sat in the dining room and jammed to blues, country and acoustic rock. The others let the talk take them down numerous roads. The kids went outside for a game of tag, the cat found a lap, the newborn slept and the sun slipped behind the mountain to the west. The snowy platter of the lake turned purple in the gathering dark. Later, there was tea and cookies, along with the crackle of a fire in the woodstove.

When we left, finally, it was to hugs and handshakes, smiles and laughter. Deb and I walked to the car with full stomachs and light hearts, feeling the glow that comes from good times in the company of good friends. When we got back to our own home, I saw it as a living thing, containing its own stories, carrying the spirit of the lives it holds between its walls. Walking through the door to the welcome of the dog, I stood for a moment and just looked at everything.

Deb and I come from broken homes. Both of us were put up for adoption when we were small, and the families we landed in were ill suited to the people we were meant to be. No one took the time to get to know us. Instead, they set out to make us exactly like them. Our days were marked by rigid discipline, neglect and loneliness. The gatherings we experienced back then were mostly about exclusion and separateness. It's taken us both a long time to get over that. We became loners because of those unwelcoming family circles, more comfortable without company than with it, happier in a small, well-chosen circle of associates than in a gregarious crowd. We lived in the corners of rooms, at the fringes of things. But here at the lake we've learned what it feels like to be included.

It's the land that connects us. I'm convinced of that. Everyone around us is here because the land has a song we want to listen to through every season, in all kinds of weather. We're a motley Canadian crew: Ukrainian, Ojibway, Scots, French, Cree and Scandinavian. We live in community, allowing each other our privacy but gathering, at times like this, for the ceremony of togetherness. We enter our homes filled with it, are framed by it, with its power to erase tattered histories and soothe ragged souls. We are framed by it, buoyed by it, this deeply spiritual sense that is far more than the effect of geography.

This is our home and native land, and we belong here—all of us. There's a miracle that's put into motion by the opening of a door and a hearty welcome, whatever language that welcome is spoken in.

The Power of Stories

IN THE EARLY fall of 2009, Deb and I travelled to Prince George, B.C., for the Aboriginal Storytellers and Writers Festival. It's a gathering of people who consider creating and sharing stories central to their lives. There are quite a few such gatherings for First Nations writers now, and every year more are added to my itinerary. That's good to see. It means there's a strong forward motion in the development of Aboriginal literature, and I'm proud to be a small part of that.

I've learned a lot about storytelling in the last thirty years. I've been privileged to learn from some great old-time story-tellers and to share time with accomplished Native writers who come from that tradition. Since I was twenty-eight, my life has been guided by the example of those writers and the vision of those traditional storytellers. Whenever I stand at a podium I feel honoured to be included in such august company.

At the Prince George festival, I shared the stage with the novelist Eden Robinson and poets Garry Gottfriedson and Duncan Mercredi. We were Ojibway, Secwepemc, Haida and Metis. There was a good-sized crowd on hand to hear us read, and the response was enthusiastic. It wasn't all that long ago that there were no published Native writers, so it was encouraging to see so many people there.

The work we presented that day ranged widely. While I listened to my peers, it struck me again how vital storytelling is to everyone. Everybody is keen on a good story well told. It's one of the things we have in common as humans. No matter how many things change in the world around us, our fascination with stories will remain. We've been sharing them forever.

A few weeks after the festival, yet another truth about stories revealed itself to me.

Vaughan Begg and Blanca Schorcht have been friends of ours for more than six years now. They stood up for us at our wedding, and the four of us love and respect each other. They live in Quesnel, a four-hour drive from where we are, and the distance affects our ability to get together regularly. But when we do, it's as if there was never any time apart, and the talk is lively. We all share a love of music, books, skiing, the outdoors and the feel of home wrapped around us. Vaughan and Blanca are also the kind of friends who know intuitively how much you're ready to share about certain things. They respect boundaries and are willing to wait without judgement until you're ready to open up.

On the last day of a recent visit, we went for a long hike into the back country. We followed a steep, winding trail to a place where an ancient waterfall had gouged eerie channels through about a hundred metres of rock. There were wide pools and small rapids where the water coursed down. It was awesome. Then we hiked back out, grabbed some ingredients for supper and settled in with music and conversation once we got back to their house.

The meal was special, but once the dishes had been cleared, a fantastic argument got underway. It began with us griping about computers and their role in the workplace. All of us had experienced difficulty with IT personnel, and the grousing soon turned to that issue. As a former systems analyst, Deb had her view. Vaughan's views as a network user were equally firm. The words flew around the kitchen table. Points were made; points were rebutted. It was a good, fiery battle, and in the end there was no clear winner.

Sometimes I back away when an argument gets heated, even when it involves people I trust. My fear of conflict is residue from when I was a kid and was allowed no voice and given no credit for my opinions or thoughts. Many times when I was young, I watched arguments boil over and become really nasty. That taught me to be careful. But watching my wife and my friend have it out that night, I saw how things could be different. Under the right circumstances, you can put on the gloves and slug it out verbally without anybody getting hurt. You can present your best thinking, your nurtured viewpoint and balance those against some one else's ideas without provoking open warfare.

The respectful exchange that evening was possible because of stories. The four of us have taken the time to show each other who we are. We've shared the stories of our lives, and that's why there's no pressure to win when arguments break out. Instead, there's respect for someone's experience and outlook, the joy of getting to know that person even better through the exchange of ideas.

Our stories don't have to be elaborate or highly dramatic to be powerful—they just have to be about us. When we share them with others, we let ourselves be known and understood. We build strong relationships in which respect is front and centre. Once this respect is established, all of our interactions are an opportunity for growth—even a good, rip-roaring argument.

Street Gangs

I **WAS IN** a street gang once, in a time so far removed it feels like another life. It was 1973, and I was seventeen. Our world was rock 'n' roll, tight jeans and T-shirts, Earth shoes, lava lamps and soft drugs. Flower Power reigned, and there was a charm to being a member of the counterculture. Peace signs proliferated. If you were a "head" in those days you were a hippie, a raging addict bent on robbery.

There were ten of us in our gang, and we called ourselves the Freaks. The Freaks weren't feared by anyone. Nor did the police pay us any more attention than a casual wave of the hand to clear us off the steps of the old courthouse in St. Catharines where we congregated. The music we loved brought us together. The Beatles had just disbanded. Jimi, Janis and Jim were dead. Pink Floyd's *Dark Side of the Moon* was required listening, as were Neil Young's *Time Fades Away* and the Rolling Stones' *Goats Head Soup.* These purple summer evenings seemed to last forever.

The Freaks were a bunch of teenagers who had fled our homes because of family breakdown, domestic violence or abuse. There was nowhere to go but the streets of our city. We were a gang only in the very loosest terms. We were

school dropouts, poor and mostly unemployed, a motley collection of lost souls who clung to each other for community.

Ticket prices were still reasonable for rock concerts then.
We would pool our money and go to shows at Buffalo's Rich
Stadium, Hamilton's Ivor Wynne Stadium, Maple Leaf Gar-
dens in Toronto and the Forum in Montreal. We saw Pink
Floyd, Led Zeppelin, the Stones, the Who, Neil Young, the
Allman Brothers and a host of other music giants. We made
the trip to and from these events in a variety of dilapidated
vans and station wagons. Sleeping bodies lay every which
way inside these cars. We'd missed Woodstock, but we were
determined to be anywhere music raised its long-haired head.

Back at the pavilion at St. Catharines' Montebello Park, we
drank cheap wine and listened to music on portable 8-track
players. We never caused a ruckus, and the police were content to let us be. We played Frisbee. We shared our food and
our cash and crashed on each others' couches when we were
lucky enough to have them.

The Night Stalkers, a local car club, were moneyed kids
from the west side. They were the cheerleaders and quarter-
backs, class presidents and valedictorians. They drove around
in fancy, tricked-out cars with the name of their "gang" in
glittery script on the bumpers. The Night Stalkers were shiny
and beautiful. They gleamed in comparison to us. Whenever
they drove past, they would blare their horns and yell taunts
at us. They laughed openly at our rust-bucket cars when we
could afford the gas to cruise around in them.

Because we were all teenagers, we'd inevitably end up
at the some of the same places. The main one was the roller
skating rink, the social-networking site of the day. The music
was loud, the food was cheap. The rink was also the only
place where the Freaks could outshine the Night Stalkers. We

were more adventurous skaters, more daring, and we lived for rhythm and abandon to the beat. In our rented skates, we skated rings around our rivals.

Now and then, there'd be fights in the parking lot. The combatants who squared off generally ended up with nothing more than a bloody nose or a black eye. After the fight, both sides would disappear to celebrate or to grouse, depending on the outcome. There was never a rumble or a riot.

One by one, the Freaks got jobs, settled into relationships or left town. The Night Stalkers drifted off to university or college. Our harmless teenage tribalism had marked none of us. It was a stark contrast to the gang era we live in now.

Aboriginal gangs flourish today in the concrete rez of Canada's prisons, the low-income neighbourhoods of cities and in reserve communities themselves. They emulate the big-city gangs of the United States with their tattoos, their graffiti, their clothing, their music, their gang signs and their violence. They proclaim themselves as warriors, but there's nothing warrior-like about them. In Native tradition, a warrior is honoured for living a principled life, standing up for the people and working to sustain them. There is none of that in an Aboriginal gang. Nor is there any true Native pride, just a dismal caricature and the costly struggle to maintain it. Lives are lost, homes disrupted, communities destroyed. These gangs are a blight, yet our Native politicians seldom mention them. They rarely talk about those slain in random shootings and knifings or those lost to addiction, prostitution or prison. They remain quiet about the sad irony of our own people killing and oppressing each other. They don't mention the kids who've had their childhoods taken away.

We need a gang mentality to offset gang mentality. We need the whole gang of us, this community of human beings, to reach back into the traditional teachings of our cultures and pass those principles on to our youth. They are our future. They are the future of the planet, and they need our input and our guiding energy if they are to assume control of our human destiny with dignity and pride. It's not just a Native thing—it's a human thing. The trick, in the end, is that by teaching them we reaffirm the same teachings for ourselves. The whole gang of us moving forward in peace.

How to Change the World

AN ELDER FRIEND once taught me something crucial about
how to change the world. I was in my early thirties, just
becoming politically active in pursuit of Native rights. By
then, my comprehension of Native issues had grown to
encompass the environment, hunting, education, employment, spiritual empowerment and the use of traditional
science, a list far beyond treaty rights, land claims and constitutional issues.

The elder and I were walking by a river as we visited.
Her name was Lorraine Sinclair. She'd founded the Mother
Earth Healing Society, an organization seeking to build
a diverse community of people around the desire to return
the planet to balance and harmony. She was recognized as a
wise and learned woman, and I sought her advice often. That
day, I described my frustration at pushing forward our people's agenda. The magnitude of the issues was daunting. As
a journalist, I feared my work would never be finished. We
were beset by far more problems than there were practical
solutions, it seemed, and the situation was agonizing and
exhausting.

Lorraine listened attentively, as she always did. We
walked a long way along that river, and I waited as patiently

as I could for her words. I expected her to prop me up, to offer praise for my efforts. I expected to leave with an emotional and spiritual band-aid firmly in place. What I got from her was far more.

As we paused by a pool in the river, Lorraine took up a pebble and tossed it in. In silence, we watched the ripples eddy outward in concentric rings and lap the stones at our feet. "That's the way you change the world," she said. "The smallest circles first."

Creator built us of energy and spirit. Beneath our flesh and bones are molecules, atoms and neutrons spinning in a nonstop cosmic dance. That is the truth of our physical reality, so one small act can have wide-ranging consequences. That's what she showed me. Do what you can where you can. Think less of the big picture than of what is achievable right now. Do whatever needs doing with a grateful heart and a mind clear of expectation. That's how you change the world.

Almost a quarter of a century later, I'm still pondering her message. I thought of Lorraine's words again not long ago, in connection with a new tradition Deb and I have started at our house. It's really an old tradition that we've dusted off and revived. It's a ritual that hearkens back to the days when people would gather in their homes to tell stories, read to each other and sing songs. It predates television, computers and cell phones.

We share a potluck dinner first. We never ask anyone to bring a particular dish; we're grateful for whatever arrives. The night of our first gathering, we had an incredible feast. Everywhere you looked there were people talking and eating and having a great time. When the meal was over, the main event got started. I walked around with an old hat, and everyone who chose to dropped in a slip of paper with their name on it. After Debra and I had welcomed everybody and sung a song, we drew the first name out of the hat, and that person sat in our antique rocker and did her thing. There were eighteen of us that night. Deb and I had invited a few friends, and they had spread the word, so the people who came were mostly strangers to us and each other. But there was a feeling of safety and community in our living room that night.

Everyone had the chance to tell a story, sing a song, read something they'd written, read something that had moved them or introduce a special piece of recorded music. We sat in candlelight, with the fire in the woodstove crackling, and we were awed by what came out.

We heard a touching story about homelessness and setting down roots from a man who lives down the way. He and I had never spoken before, only nodded at each other when we passed on the road. But his words were riveting. They showed him to be a man with a history much like mine. Without that gathering, I might never have had the privilege of learning that. We listened to folk songs performed on a six-string guitar and a blues song accompanied only by hand claps. People told stories about childhood, the spirituality of fly fishing and the trials of war. One person read a poem for the earth.

As the evening progressed, people sank deeper into their chairs. The silence between offerings was an oration in itself. There was no need for booze, loud music, video games or other contemporary distractions. Instead, we luxuriated in the old-time feeling of togetherness.

Deb and I have held similar gatherings every month since. Everyone who comes leaves feeling more complete, more attuned to their neighbours. Community happens that way, people coming together for a common purpose. That's what Lorraine meant when she said "the smallest circles first." One ripple at a time: that's how we will change the world.

What Marriage Means

I WAS TWENTY-FOUR the first time I got married. I had no clear idea at the time of where I wanted my life to go, and I hoped my wife would to be an anchor holding me in place long enough for that realization to come. But that's not the role of a wife, and we were battling the crippling disease of my alcoholism then, too. I hadn't suffered enough yet to want to get sober. I still believed that I was young and indestructible and that life would always throw new beginnings at me. I thought drinking was manly. I thought everyone drank the same way I did.

My first wife was an artist, a dancer. She sparkled with energy, and that was what drew me to her. As long as I was in her company, I believed that I would sparkle, too. Sometimes it worked; I would flare and accomplish great things. But the depth of my shadow self was always stronger. Eventually I exhausted her patience and her faith. We were divorced in absentia, because she didn't know where I was.

When I married the second time, I was forty-three. I'd had periods of sobriety by then, some as long as a year, but I still didn't understand that my drinking was the symptom of a greater ill. I'd become an award-winning newspaper columnist, a television writer and host and a first-time novelist. But the wounds that drove me to push for success also drove me to alcohol. I thought that love could save me. I thought that the magic of romance would rescue me. I was drunk when I met my second wife for the first time, and I was drunk when I said "I do." There was never any hope for that union. It ended quickly and bitterly.

Now, at fifty-four, I have a productive, creative life rooted to a home in the mountains and a woman who is my best friend. I don't drink anymore. I found people to help me. I looked under the bed and confronted the monsters that lurked there and took away their power. I spend a lot of time now trying to help others find their own way to grace. By helping them, I help myself.

Debra has never tried to save me. When I fell, she was strong enough to let me flail until I found my footing again. She fought her own battle with the bottle and has been sober now for almost a decade. Watching her, I found the example I needed. She is resilient. Iron-willed. Grateful for being on this earth. Committed to a life that has no room for booze, for self-inflicted misery or ghosts. What I saw in her, I wanted for myself. Bit by bit, I laboured toward the same place.

Love is not about rescue, I understand now—it's about allowing. In the Ojibway world, love is the process of you leading me back to who I am. You do that by stepping back and allowing the creative, nurturing energy of the universe to work. That's the most courageous thing you can do when you love somebody. Deb showed me that. Both of us knew we'd found communion with one another. We're loyal to the vision of our togetherness.

When Deb and I decided to get married, we held the ceremony in our yard. In the beginning, we'd envisioned a small wedding with a few close friends. But as word got out, we got phone calls and emails from people requesting invitations. In the end, on that spectacular sunny day in July, there were fifty of us. Some people had come a long way. Some were from our community at the lake, and others made the short drive from Kamloops. A good friend who is a marriage commissioner performed the ceremony. Deb and I read the vows we had written. We stood in the midst of that circle of people who love us and became husband and wife. Later, we shared a potluck meal, a homemade wedding cake, music and the joy of being connected in the energy of something special.

We exchanged rings in the ceremony, but we also tied eagle feathers together. To me, those feathers stand for commitment. They are a symbol of the courage that allowed me to change my life and the courage that allows me to continue on this path. They are symbols of honour and justice, of the coming together of equals. They are a symbol of faith, the act of believing in the grace and love of a higher being, a God, a Creator, a Great Spirit. The feathers are something of my culture I value highly. They are an outward sign of the depth of the vows I took that day.

Being a husband is an honour and a responsibility. The ring on my finger reminds me of that. The eagle feathers that hang in our house exemplify it. They are strong in themselves, but they are made stronger by virtue of being tied together. This time around, the word "husband" means something very special to me.

Families

TOLSTOY WROTE THAT all happy families are alike, but each unhappy family is unhappy in its own way. I'm not familiar with the details of Russian family life in the 1800s, but I know that Count Leo was on to something. I've been around for over half a century now. I've spent time in hundreds of homes and witnessed thousands of interactions between people bound by blood. I've been in homes where silence rules and anger simmers under everything. I've visited families whose simple, abundant love for each other fills me with awe. Good or bad, they've all taught me something.

At our home in the mountains, my family consists of Debra and me, Molly the dog and a host of friends. My extended family is huge now. As a good friend puts it, I have a big chosen family.

I was separated from my Native family as a toddler. For years, I had no idea where I came from or who my people were. When I reconnected with them twenty-four years later, we had to get to know each other again. Each of us had experienced a lot of pain in our lives, and a lot of broken trust. We bore all of that back into the mix, so our time together was often pretty glum.

Life with my adopted family was horrendous. As staunch, strict Presbyterians, they knew nothing about Native history, spirituality, tradition or culture. They knew nothing of the abuse I'd already suffered. Their efforts to make me fit their ideal filled me with anger and resentment, and I ran away as soon as I could.

When I married my first wife, I was introduced to an extraordinary family of people who genuinely cared about each other. They accepted me as one of them, and for a time I felt as though I actually belonged somewhere. When my marriage ended because of my alcoholism, I mourned the loss of that family as deeply as I mourned the loss of my wife.

I've visited homes that had great fist-sized holes in the walls. I've also had friends and lovers whose family homes were obsessively ordered and immaculate. In those homes, I was never sure where to place my feet, and the conversation was as stiff as the plastic on the sofa. Recently, Deb and I sat on our deck talking with a good friend. He's South African by birth. He's not someone you'd categorize as conflicted if you saw him on the street. He's trim and fit with an open face and an engaging manner. He's terrifically funny, whip-smart, open-minded, adventurous, opinionated and engaged with the world. When he told us his story of growing up, I was dumbfounded.

Our friend described a great gulf between brothers created by extraordinary differences in their worldviews and their approach to living. He told us about physical, mental, emotional and spiritual damage that had created gaps seemingly impossible to bridge. Maybe it was the shadow of apartheid he grew up in, or maybe it was just the natural separation that occurs in families as we grow, but he sensed the rift and felt helpless to bridge it. His people felt like strangers to him and to each other, he said. He reflected on his family's lack of real conversation, their inability to express any emotion other than anger, the loneliness he had felt in that house. He talked quietly, bearing the weight of his story on his shoulders.

When there's pain in our lives, we tend to believe that we're the only ones. Often we keep that pain to ourselves out of embarrassment or shame. But when we do that, we put ourselves out of the reach of those who might help us. As I listened to my friend's story, feeling waves of empathy, understanding and compassion flow through me, I realized again that we can create family with anyone. We all need a place to share, and it's through sharing and listening that we heal.

When my people say that it takes a community to raise a child, they mean a group of spirits working in concert. They mean a people committed to honouring the individual and, consequently, to honouring all. They mean the human family. All of us are members, and we owe it to each other to respect and honour that.

WEST

INTROSPECTION

ON THE MEDICINE Wheel, introspection is the "looks within place." Humility and trust offer many teachings, and introspection is a means of seeing how those apply to our lives. It's a place of vision. It's a resting place where the story, the song each of us has created up to this moment can be inspected and those things deemed unnecessary be let go. It's a place of courage, because the hardest place to look is within. Many people stop here, deterred by the trials of the journey and the sudden hurts that sometimes make life hard. But introspection is meant to bring us to balance. It is the place where all things are ordered, where all things ring true at the same time. Balance allows us to move forward, and when we do, the journey becomes wondrous again by virtue of our ability to see the whole trail.

Impossible Blue

THERE'S A SPECIAL shade of blue that appears where the sun meets the horizon every morning. It sits in that mysterious space where darkness meets light, where night begins its brightening into day. My people call this time of day *Beedahbun*, first light, but there's no word for that particular colour, an off-purple fading into blue grey. You need to sacrifice some sleep and comfort in order to be out under the sky when that colour emerges, and not many people are motivated to do it. That's sad. For me, that colour is gateway to the spiritual realm.

I discovered that for the first time in 1985, when I was one of a group of aspiring storytellers gathered on Manitoulin Island. We had gone there for ten days to sit with elders, hear traditional stories and teachings and figure out how to incorporate those into our contemporary work in theatre, fiction and poetry.

The elders told us on the first night that it was the desire, the yearning we carried, that would make all things possible. The elders were so calm. They felt so grounded. When they walked, they seemed to move in a shroud of silence. I wanted that depth of connection to myself and to the world, so I was determined to listen carefully and follow their directions.

One of the first things they instructed us to do was to get ourselves outside early in the morning. We weren't supposed to use an alarm clock or ask anyone else to ensure that we woke. Instead, we were to harness our desire and use that energy to get us up on time—to intuit when the time was right. Those instructions felt strange to me then. I was struggling hard to survive in my city life, and I wasn't used to integrating traditional teachings. This would be my first real test. The elders wanted us to face east as first light came up over the trees. We were to sit there without speaking and watch, then later to tell them the story of what we saw there.

The first morning was chilly. It was late October, frosty, the taste of snow in the wind and a scrim of ice at the edge of the small lake. It was hard sitting on a cold rock waiting for first light to break. I'd had no coffee, and the clothes I'd brought were insufficient for the season. I was very cold. But I made myself stay there and wait for something to occur.

At first I saw nothing. Then I began to discern swirls and shapes in the sky. As the sun emerged, a wild palette of colours I had never imagined spread slowly across the skyline. Time slipped away, as did the discomfort I'd been feeling.

I was awestruck when I first spotted that impossible blue. I recognized it immediately, not as a memory but as an ache at my very centre. That incandescence awoke something inside of me, and when I felt it stir to life I wanted to cry.

When I described this to the elders later, they smiled. They explained that special colour represents both emptiness and fullness; it carries the possibility of everything. When the universe was created, it contained both those properties. So do our spirits when we are born. But as life happens, we gradually shut that boundless possibility down. Rules and judgement cause it to shrink. The storyteller in all of us can go into hiding, lying dormant within us. When I saw that special blue, my storytelling spirit was sparked to life again.

Over the next nine days, the elders showed me how to coax a flame from that ember of spirit. They told us about the rich protocol and traditions of storytelling. We talked about how vital stories and storytellers were to the lifeblood of our people at one time and how urgent it was for us to bring that vitality back in whatever creative form we chose to use. And every morning, I took myself outside, sat on that rock and watched the light break across the sky.

It's twenty-four years later, and now I'm a seasoned story-teller myself. I've tried to integrate everything those elders taught me into a body of work that gets bigger each year. As often as I can, I get up in front of people and use the ancient tools. I connect to that impossible blue that lives within me, that area of both fullness and emptiness, and then I speak.

The Loon's Necklace

THE CALL OF the loon, the great bird known as Mong in
Ojibway, is heard throughout Ojibway territory. That call is
so piercing and strong that in the Ojibway clan system, the
Loon Clan carries the responsibility for chieftainship. Some
people say that the loon is also a symbol of communication
and of family. When you see a female loon on the water in
the spring and early summer, with her babies on her back as
she swims, you can easily see why.

The loon's call is haunting and wild, an ancient trill that's
part honour song and part warning. I've never met anyone
who didn't fall quiet upon hearing it. We're all susceptible to
that common magic.

There is a traditional story about a man who had grown
very old. He had lost his vision, which meant he could no longer hunt or fish to take care of his family. This knowledge
made him sad. The man sat at the edge of the water one day,
shedding tears. The ripples they created attracted a loon, who
swam close to shore to investigate.

"Why are you crying?" the loon asked the old man.

"Oh, great loon," the old man said. "Your red eyes are
bright, and you can dive to find fish in the depths of the water.

My eyes have grown dim, and my family is hungry. That is why I'm crying."

"Take hold of my wings," the loon said to the old man. "Hold very tight, and I will dive to the deepest part of the lake, where the water is purest. When we surface, you will be able to see again."

The old man grasped the loon's wings tightly, and the bird dove. Down and down she swam, to where the water was very cold and dark. The old man thought his lungs would burst. But he held on tight, as the loon had told him to do. Eventually the loon crested the surface, and the old man found he could make out the blurred outlines of trees and rock. They dove again. The old man was tired. His grasp loosened, and he was afraid he would slip off the loon's back and drown. But he held fast, and the next time they broke the surface he could see clearly.

The man was overjoyed. He hugged the loon and cried tears of gratitude. "I am so grateful," he said. "I will make you a gift of my most prized possession."

The man was wearing a necklace of sacred white shells. He removed it, then placed it around the loon's neck. In those times, the loon's feathers were pure black. Everywhere the shells touched her, though, her feathers turned white. Through her compassion for the old man, the loon got the white necklace and the white pattern on her back we see today.

Shortly after I had reconnected with my Native family, I stood in the darkness one evening on a northern beach with my uncle Archie. Arch had been a bushman all his life. He'd worked along Winnipeg River as a fishing guide, hunting guide and trapper. It was midsummer, and the sky was clear, filled with a million stars. As we watched for meteors, Arch told me how the constellations were named for the animals the Ojibway saw on their journeys. Then we heard a loon call. The sound wobbled out of the darkness and died out in echoes across the water. After a long silence, the call came again.

My uncle cupped his hands and blew into them. I'd never heard anyone do a pitch-perfect loon call before, and in a few seconds the loon responded from across the water. Arch cupped his hands again and blew another series of trills and dips. Again, the loon responded.

As they called back and forth, the loon drew closer to us. We could hear the bird approaching. I waited to see if my uncle would call the loon right to the beach, but he stopped suddenly and put hands in his pockets. There was silence then, as thick as the night. I imagined the loon swimming away in the darkness. I could see the outline of my uncle, his face tilted up towards the sky.

When I asked him why he'd stopped calling, he took his time answering. He sat down on the beach, and I sat down beside him. When he spoke again, his voice was hushed. "The loon calls to remind us that everything is alive," he said. "A loon's call reminds us to look outside ourselves, at the air, the land, the water, and brings us back into the natural order of things. There's no need to see the teacher. We only need to feel the teaching."

People pay big money trying to get to the heart of Native traditions. There are hucksters and sham artists everywhere adorned with Aboriginal motifs. The truth, though, is that the teachings are available to everyone. All we need to do is pay attention, and be open to them when they arrive. Next time you hear a loon, remember that.

The Puzzle

I'VE ALWAYS BEEN a thinker. As a kid, I sought explanations for even the simplest things around me. The adults I asked never seemed adequately armed, so I dove into the pages of books. I wanted to know how birds migrated without a compass, what made rain happen, why the planets move in ellipses. I sought answers to a plethora of questions about the world.

Age is a curious thing. As you mature, the questions that occupy you become more onerous. Queries about the natural world are replaced with harder questions like who should I be, how do I get there, why do people suffer and how do things change? These questions are so big that we tend to forget the reassurance that comes from simple answers.

I once asked a friend how he thought we should go about changing the world. How can we address the myriad issues that threaten us as a species? How could I, as someone just beginning to feel empowered as a First Nations man, find a way to improve the lot of my people? How could I get beyond the turmoil and struggles of my own life to help someone else? This was heady stuff, and I prepared myself for a long, challenging discussion. But what my friend said floored me.

As a self-employed contractor, my friend worked at home. His wife had a job outside the home, so he looked after their ten-year-old son after school. Once he'd picked his son up, fed him a snack and spent some play time with him, my friend would get back to work. Usually the boy would do his homework or amuse himself in his room. But one afternoon, on a day that was particularly hectic for my friend, the boy desperately wanted more of his father's attention.

So my friend ripped a picture out of a magazine, a photo that showed the world from outer space. He tore the picture into tiny pieces, handed them to the boy and asked his son to put the picture back together. Thinking the assigned task would take forever, my friend settled into his work. But his son was back in five minutes, with the puzzle solved and glued to a piece of paper.

"How did you do that so fast?" he asked the boy.

"Simple," the boy said. "There was a picture of a man on the other side. So I put the man together first, and the world came together just fine."

That simple parable from daily life has been a saving grace for me ever since. Put the man together first, and the world will come together just fine.

The enormity of the world's problems can feel overwhelming. Resolution can seem impossible. But when we join together wholeheartedly, when the energy we put forward is calm, positive and centred, great change is possible. I've seen it work in my own life, and I've seen it work out in the world.

My people say that change is the fundamental law of the universe. Like the weather, it happens without any input from us. But we make change, too. We just need to do it one small piece at a time.

Reigniting the Spark

WHEN I WAS small, the world seemed pretty frightening. As a foster kid, and later an adopted one, I never felt like my feet were solidly on the ground. Kids know automatically when they're being excluded. You get a bruised feeling in your chest that never really goes away. But there isn't a time I can remember when the natural world didn't offer something that captivated me, whether it was a cave buried in a cliff or a rushing river churning itself into rapids. It might have been the Indian in me that responded so strongly to those things. But I believe we're all born with an inherent sense of wonder, and there's nothing so devastating as losing it.

Not so long ago, some Ojibway people from a remote reserve in Ontario invited me to their community. My assignment was to introduce the members of their adult education class to traditional oral storytelling skills. The students were a small group of young people for whom public high school had been a failed experiment. They hadn't been able to achieve their potential there, for one reason or another, and the band was encouraging them all to get enough credits to earn their Grade 12.

Just like the natural world, stories and storytelling have always been infused with a wild degree of mystery and magic for me. I am constantly amazed at the nature of the creative process—creating something from nothing, bringing people, places and ideas to life. And as a First Nations person, I'm constantly floored by the richness of my oral tradition. I feel the ancient thrum of it in my chest. When I write, even though I compose my words on a keyboard, nothing feels finished until I've read it aloud to myself, given it the freedom of the air. When I read my work aloud, I feel closely connected to a vibrant storytelling tradition.

I sought to bring that keen thrill to those students. I sought to ignite an ember from the old tribal fires that burned in our villages in that classroom so that we could all draw strength and inspiration. But it was not to be. The students ranged in age from nineteen to twenty-two. They'd been out of school for a handful of years, and more than half of them already had children of their own. They were all more comfortable with computer games, music videos and satellite television than they were with their own cultural heritage.

Of all the things that a history of displacement takes away from people, the sense of wonder is the harshest loss of all. After we'd walked to a small lake on a brilliant November morning, I asked the students to find a private spot for themselves, to close their eyes, breathe deep, feel that morning around them and then tell the others in the group what they felt. Not one of them could do it. Instead, they engaged in horseplay, called out to each other expressing derision for the exercise. They missed the experience of that lake in the morning sun. Little wonder they had nothing to say about it.

Later, when I did my storytelling show for the whole community, only twenty of seven hundred on-reserve residents showed up. Of those, only a few caught the wild hilarity of my stories highlighting the gamut of the Native experience.

in Canada. The others sat squinting, unmoving, unsure what to make of this strange man cavorting in front of them. Putting on that performance was hard work, and when it was over I felt very sad.

The disconnectedness in that community didn't lie just with the youth. It was all-pervasive. Life for the residents of that reserve had become drudgery, offering no hope for something different, no glinting light at the horizon. They couldn't feel amazement at the magnificent place they called home. When you lose your sense of wonder, you're incapable of seeing the magic everywhere in the world around you. The spark igniting the ingenuity, creativity and imagination that mark us as a species has been extinguished.

We can all relate to that feeling to some degree. Our day-in, day-out routines sometimes get us down. But for many of Canada's First Nations people on remote reserves, the malaise feels chronic, self-perpetuating and final.

Wonder is what fuels us, what propels us to achieve. We need the light of our imaginations to make life worth living. When Native leaders identify their people's most pressing issues, reigniting that sense of wonder should be foremost. We need to bring our people back from the inside out. Everyone deserves to experience the magic of a lake in the morning.

The Never-ending Story

EVERY MORNING, THE dog and I come back from our walk reinvigorated. We've trekked that road hundreds of times, and each trip is different. The light, the wind, an animal or two, migrating birds, trees in each new season: it's kaleidoscopic. Walking on the land is a rush to the senses when you're open to it. Each day reveals something new.

I've been a journalist for more than thirty years. I got my first reporting job in the spring of 1979, with a Native newspaper called the *New Breed* in Regina. I was a rookie, but I fell in love with the work. Since then I've expanded to radio and television and published a couple of non-fiction books. For the most part, it's been an incredible journey.

But not always. My primary focus through all of that time has been First Nations issues. I was there when Native people sat down at a negotiating table with the prime minister and the premiers for the first time in 1982. I saw hope build in relation to those constitutional talks, and I saw it crumble when we returned home without a gain after three rounds. I witnessed a pope's visit to a remote northern community. I've reported from behind barricades, covered protests, interviewed militants. I've spoken to wise and gentle elders. I've talked with medicine people and spiritual teachers. I've written about the birth of our national Native television network, the creation of an Aboriginal category at the JUNO awards and the emergence of Native role models in the arts, education, science and technology.

North, east, west and south: I've covered all of those cardinal points on the great wheel of the news. I've been proud to write about the forward and upward motion of my people. I've been empowered by their determination, pluck and resistance.

But there was always the other side, too. Over the past thirty years, I've done stories about suicide, alcoholism, drug abuse, domestic violence, the high rate of Native incarceration, the rise of street gangs, the loss of our traditional languages, the effects of residential schools and the urgent need for true leadership. In that sense, the journey hasn't been so incredible.

When I left active journalism in 1993, it was because I'd grown tired of writing the same never-ending story. Sure, there were highlights, stories that showed how far we'd come as a people, but the heart-wrenching stories repeated in a nightmarish loop, as if in a broken news reel. For every groundbreaking venture, there was a deeply discouraging step back. For every new hero, there was another faceless victim. It became too difficult to witness the process over and over again.

Sitting on my couch a few evenings ago, watching the news, I was reminded how little has changed. I sat near tears listening to the story of a young Ojibway boy on a Manitoba First Nation who had died in a house fire—a house he shared with ten others, eight of them under the age of six. A nine-year-old girl had died in a fire on the same reserve months earlier. The house she died in was shared by fourteen people. The news footage showed the dilapidated houses on either side of the destroyed one. They were not much more than shacks, but that was the housing the people of the Sandy Bay community were forced to live in. The images were stark, and I'd seen them many times before.

In the early 1980s I travelled with a Native politician named Murray Hamilton to visit some of his constituents in northern Saskatchewan. The living conditions on that reserve were horrendous. There was plastic nailed over many window frames. Thirteen people were crammed into one two-room shack with little furniture. Water had to be hauled from the nearby creek in nineteen-litre lard pails. I remembered that visit as I watched the story about the fire in Sandy Bay.

In 2009, the federal government announced that it had committed $400 million to address the crisis in Native housing. To the average person, that sounds like a lot of money, but it's not. With 640 First Nations communities across Canada, it amounts just over $600,000 per community. The size of the average single family home in Canada is 1,400 square feet, and the average cost of building it is $175 a square foot. So the average home costs $235,000 to build. That works out to just over two homes per First Nations community. When you factor in Department of Indian Affairs administration costs and the extra transportation expenditures for travelling to remote communities, that goes down to just one home per reserve.

Clearly, change is desperately needed. Not just from the federal government, but from First Nations politicians, too. We should not hear about this Aboriginal housing crisis only when tragedy happens. We shouldn't have to wait until someone dies before all Canadians hear about conditions in Kispiox, Shammattawa, Pikangikum or Attawapiskat.

Every national Aboriginal organization has a communications department. When a crisis occurs, they issue press releases clamouring for government action and enlisting public sympathy. They spout off about the need for change. But these organizations know about the existing situation, and they have for years. If their funding dollars were put to more efficient use, the rest of Canada would know how dire the situation is, too. Native journalists need to be out there telling these stories honestly, directly and relentlessly.

That's what it will take to change things. As a newsman for thirty years, I know how powerful a force public knowledge can be. When all Canadians understand how much their neighbours are suffering, I think they'll find the ways and means to address it. Governments will find the political will necessary to change these conditions. Our national Native organizations must lead the charge. Change, rightfully, will begin with them.

The Emergency

THE WEATHER WAS a phenomenon in the summer of 2009.
Every morning broke on a clear sky, and it seemed as if the
air hadn't moved since spring busted up the winter clouds.
The grass was brown and tinder dry. We never got a break
from the heat. Even the birds were too hot to sing by mid-
afternoon, and the stillness was eerie.

Summer has changed even in the four years we've lived
in the mountains. The change is visible in the forests ravaged
by the mountain pine beetle, the tussock moth and the spruce
beetle, as well as the depleted population of shore birds. Our
well runs lower because of the lack of rain. The level of the
lake has dropped so severely that we have to paddle the boat
out beyond the reeds to find sufficient depth to drop the
motor. The undergrowth in the woods is stunted and dry.
There's less moss than there used to be, and it's harder to find
wild mushrooms.

It's worrisome, this global warming. When I looked at
the forest that summer of 2009, I couldn't help but see fuel
for fires. As the temperature rose into the high 30s, we all
became wary. We were glued to our radios and TVs, fearing
the lightning strike or the careless camper that would turn

things into an inferno. People a short drive away were being evacuated. We could see the smoke from those fires drifting above the lakes.

People tried not to show how nervous they were. We grinned and waved at each other and fanned away at the clouds of dust from the gravel road. But you could tell the threat of a blaze rested heavy on everyone's minds. There wasn't a community anywhere in British Columbia that wasn't edgy and anxious.

When a fire broke out on a nearby mountain, our own community went on high alert. It was only six years since horrendous fires had swept through this part of the Interior, and nobody had forgotten that. When lightning struck our mountain and tell-tale spirals of smoke began to curl up, people drove down to the lakefront and planted themselves on their docks to keep an eye on the situation. We watched the choppers fill up their huge dangling buckets. We prayed silently as the spumes of water washed down over the stricken forest. A plane dumped retardant, and a chopper set down a small fire-fighting crew. We waited.

There were reports of other blazes on nearby hills. Cars and pickup trucks rumbled down the road to investigate, and people exchanged the bits of news that came back. The tension in the air crackled like the lick of flames. But no one spoke their worst fears aloud. Instead, we all got down to the business of being prepared to evacuate.

For Deb and I, those were difficult hours. The idea of losing the house we love so much to fire was hard. We'd painted the cabin a vibrant shade of red that spring, adding blue shutters and attractive tan accents. Viewed from out on the lake, our house seemed to shine on its slope between the trees. But we had to be practical, so we decided to pack emergency bags and leave them by the door in case the call came. We went through the house to gather the things we would absolutely need to survive or to start over somewhere else. We moved quietly, silenced by the gravity of the situation. I spent a lot of time just touching objects, as though I could commit them to memory through my skin.

First, we stashed the title deed, our marriage certificate, bank papers, tax stuff and working papers we could not do without. Then we saved our computer files to disk. We packed photographs and the little notes and letters we'd sent to each other. Deb put in the poems I'd written her, and I remembered the photo of her I keep in front of my computer monitor when I write. Then I took some photos of the house for insurance purposes. Debra packed a suitcase with clothes and toiletries.

Our house is filled with stuff: furniture, a stereo, the music collection that is my pride and joy, a television, artwork, books, a guitar, a keyboard and the other usual accoutrements of life. But the number of things we deemed elemental to our survival was small. They all fit into a backpack. That said something important to us.

Luckily, the fire never caught in our neck of the woods. Heavy rain arrived as if in answer to our prayers. We woke the next morning to a fresh, beautiful and familiar world. But when I noticed the bags beside the door, I offered thanks for the lesson. The world around us may alter in a thousand worrisome ways, it may threaten us with the loss of everything we own, but the elements that truly sustain us cannot be taken away. *Ahow.*

The Power in Silence

I'VE BEEN FORTUNATE in my time to meet some genuine traditional teachers. I've been further blessed to sit with them and talk, to walk with them out onto the land. Our times together were always punctuated with silences. Our talk was a sharing of the sacred breath of Creation, and silence was an act of reverence.

I never realized before then that silence is a spiritual thing. Most of my life I'd felt awkward with silence, seeking to fill gaps in talk with a quip, a rejoinder, an observation. The silence I experienced with traditional teachers were intentional breaks in thought, left there as bridges to emotion.

Like many people, I came to Native spirituality hoping to get things clarified and resolved, preferably instantaneously. I was looking for the sweat lodge, the pipe, and the traditional medicines to heal my old wounds and salve the raw spots that living had left on the surface of my being. Initially, I believed that my presence at ceremony would be enough in itself, that a morning smudge of sage or sweetgrass would elevate me easily beyond old pain and fresh hurts. I had a lot to learn.

A sweat lodge is not a band-aid. A pipe ceremony is not an aspirin. The real work of healing comes in how we apply the principles from those ceremonies in our daily lives. Nothing ever happens instantly. Most of the time we struggle to achieve our goals. It's in that struggle that warriors are born.

Silence allows you to pause and reflect. Like most people, I was hooked on *doing*. What those tribal teachers were telling me was the opposite: Be. Then become. It sounds so simple, but it flies directly in the face of everything we've been taught. If I can make more money, then I will be content. If I get a good job, then I will be secure. Once I have a solid love relationship, I will be satisfied. And on and on. Getting comfortable with silence helped me to turn all that around. Being spiritual, in the Indian way, means simply getting in touch with whatever moves your spirit. Silence is one tool I employ. A painting, a photograph, a good book, the words of a song, a blues riff, the touch of a hand, quiet talk, a walk with my dog: all of these things also move my spirit. When you learn to carry that feeling into everything you do, your life becomes a ceremony—and that's the whole intention.

Close your eyes and feel the silence. There will be lots of time for talk beyond that.

A Day of Protest

WHEN THE FIRST National Aboriginal Day was announced in 1996, I thought it was a wonderful idea. One day each year set aside for Native people to strut their stuff and be recognized for their contributions to the development of the larger nation. The day was set to coincide with the summer solstice, a time when Sun Dances are traditionally held. Those elaborate, powerful ceremonies are meant to align people's energy with the life-affirming energy of the sun. The whole thing seemed perfect. But time passed, and the political aspirations of my people continued to go unheeded by a series of governments. The horrendous social conditions on most reserves and the correlative urban issues persisted. It became apparent to Native people that a day devoted to song and dance and finery wasn't cutting it. So the National Day of Protest was born.

The first protest day was held in 2007. Except for a couple of train blockades and a few thousand disgruntled motorists, it was a non-event. When the government still failed to act on Native issues, the country's Aboriginal leaders called us out for a more sustained assault. They wanted Native people to become more vocal, more strident, more disruptive— and, in the end, more divisive. It didn't sound much like nation-building to me. To my way of thinking, our energies ought to be directed towards that. Certainly action is desperately needed to bring First Nations people into equal partnership in Canada, but we're all neighbours here. A day devoted to disruption doesn't make sense.

Here in the mountains, our community is peaceful. A protest action on my part wouldn't achieve much. There's only the one road leading to town. It's a beautiful drive, and everyone needs that road for access to groceries, water, work and entertainment. Laying my body across it as a barricade would be counterproductive. Besides, for the rednecks who are a significant part of the demographic up here, an Indian on the highway would be nothing more than a speed bump.

Then there's economic disruption. I could refuse to add my hard-earned dollars to the local white economy. I could stockpile the goods I need and remove myself from active participation in commerce. That would be fine until the buzz wore off. Contemporary Indians like me have grown too used to conveniences, and I'd have to spring for pizza and a movie at some point. Besides, taking my cash out of the mix would be like sneaking a penny out of a lard pail full of change.

I could always march. I even have a hand drum. There are warrior flags for sale almost anywhere these days, and I could walk a few yards out from my house and hew a stout sapling to hang one from. The avenues are wide in town, so I could stride the length of the main street with my drum, singing, denouncing injustice and aggravating shop owners. But there's always that dang Indian speed-bump thing.

My safest bet would be to occupy a plot of land. Surely, at some time in the primordial past, a Native person must have performed a ritual in the trees beyond our home. That would make it sacred land. I wouldn't need to prove that; Canadians, being a trusting lot, would take my word for it. I could head out there and construct a barricade from beetle-kill trees, light a sacred fire, schedule a press conference, make a big statement, wave my warrior flag and beat my hand drum. There must be an Ojibway word for photo op. I just haven't learned it yet.

I wouldn't be bored. While out there waiting for the military ouster, I could pass the time listening to jazz tunes downloaded onto my iPod. I could stay in touch with other protest actions by surfing the Internet on my BlackBerry, send messages to other warrior factions through my Facebook account and Twitter details to everyone in cyberspace. During slow periods, I could shoot a cell-phone video of me, all stoic and resentful, to upload onto YouTube.

My protest would call for some preparation, of course. If you're going to occupy land, you need the appropriate wardrobe. For Native protests these days, camouflage is the new Hilfiger. I'd also need my eyebrows done: they need to display cleanly above the camouflage bandana and the mirrored Oakley shades.

In the end, it sounds too stressful. I'd lose a few days of work. My neighbours would complain about the smoke from the sacred fire and my throat would be sore from singing late into the night. Besides, there have been so many marches, protests and barricades that they've become passé to most people. An indignant Indian is as much as a Canadian motif now as the beaver on the nickel.

No, for me the idea of protest lacks vision. My neighbours and I co-exist marvellously. We've learned to live together in a degree of harmony. There's always someone around to lend a hand. We keep an eye on each other's property. We've created a community without the need for labels and divisiveness. Everybody wants security, belonging and fellowship when they step beyond their yards.

We don't need a national day of protest. What we need is a national day of communication. We need to foster human understanding. Native people need to be good neighbours, and we need our own leaders to point us in this direction. Let's lean over the back fence and talk to each other about our lives. Let's get beyond differences, beyond rednecks, beyond stereotypes and hear each other's stories. It's not hard. As Canadians, we were raised with that small-town, do-a-favour mentality, and all we need to do is remember.

Simple, everyday acts bring people together. I don't feel much like an Indian when I walk around my community. I feel included. I feel a part of things. What it took to accomplish that was an earnest desire on my part to create a sustained front with my neighbours—and it works. That's lucky, because camouflage makes me look fat.

Now and Then

COWS HAVE WANDERED in off the rangeland. In the stillness of dawn, they are bawling from beyond the trees, and their voices are harsh against the call of loons and ducks from the water. From where I sit on the deck with my first morning coffee, the contrast between the domesticated sounds and the wild ones is captivating. The wild calls are much less fretful. No one needs to come and find those ducks in the bush.

Deb and I live in a small community of refugees from the city. Our house sprawls around the northern edge of Paul Lake, with wide expanses of fir, aspen, wild rose and lawns between them. It's urban here, almost, except that mountain and the bush loom close by. The brightness of the stars is unimpeded by the harsh glare of streetlights. Deb and I love the charm of this setting, but like everyone else we have our share of conveniences. The rooflines of our neighbours feature satellite dishes. Driveways are filled with SUVs, pickups, ATVs, dirt bikes and boats on trailers. We have high-speed Internet now out here in the sticks, and high-definition TVs for watching the big games and pay-per-view movies.

So it's heartening to hear the sound of cattle. Closing my eyes in the morning air, I imagine the Canada of yesteryear:

dust thrown up from the hoofs of horses, the slap of leather and the yip of cow dogs mixed in with the hoot and holler of cowboys. The pioneer feel of a burgeoning country isn't far away. And some actual cowboys will come for these cattle soon. It's a common enough sight out here, wranglers herding cows back to safety. Sitting loose and limber in the saddle against the backdrop of a stunning blue sky.

Native people are big on tradition. We feel pride in our tribal origins. We're big on history as the backbone of today. When we speak about the conditions of our contemporary lives, we do so in reference to earlier times. We're rightfully proud of our legends and our lore. Who we are today rests on the bedrock of our past.

It's the same with my neighbours. Ukrainian, Scots, French or English, they all have stories of their people in days gone by: winters that were harder, snows that were deeper, droughts that were more dire. They all have tales of times when things seemed simpler, when traditions were steadfastly observed and values were shared.

We're also alike in our need for reassurance. We all bear the same measure of fear and uncertainty about the enormous sweep of changes around us and its effect on our families. We just don't talk about those times much. Often it takes something big to remind us that we share the same history, feel the same attachment to our beginnings.

But the bawl of cattle from the edge of the yard can show you that, if you let it. It's the rustic heart of an older Canada, the foundation of our modern life.

Our country is a great aggregate of races and cultures. Recognizing that is what will help us to heal and to move closer together. *Ahow.*

Writing Space

EVER SINCE I began to write professionally, I've wanted a writing space. I did my work in any number of cubicles, offices and odd corners over the years. Some of my novels were written at kitchen tables. One memoir was finished in the health office on my mother's reserve. A section of my novel *Ragged Company* was written on the beach beside a mountain lake. But I never had a private place to write until now.

When we bought our cabin, Deb and I knew there were a lot of things that needed fixing. The old bachelor who had built the place had let it run down over time. Bit by bit, we got to work. The thing that seemed hardest to tackle was the old garage, so we left it to last.

The garage was large and musty, badly lit with a pocked concrete floor, no heating or insulation, and a weird little addition tacked on. The walls had been fashioned from assorted pieces of castoff plywood. The picture window looking out at the lake was a single pane of glass with a few years of dust built up on it. There also was a hinged window, ten centimetres high by 1.5 metres wide. We wondered about that until a neighbour told us old Walter would push wood through that window, then cut it on his table saw. The garage was jammed with junky cabinets and a huge pile of the sawn barn timbers the old man had used for firewood.

Mice, pack rats and other critters had used the huge gaps in the garage's foundation to gain entry. The sliding garage door was dented, and a quirky little handmade door was just wide enough for one person to get through.

It looked like the project from hell. But Deb wanted a studio where she could do her fused glass designs. She'd trundled the kiln, glass and the assorted tools around for years, without an appropriate place to put them, and she saw potential in that garage. As we attended to the cabin's more glaring needs, and burned off that huge pile of wood in the garage, our ideas for changing the space blossomed. As soon as we could afford the materials, we set out to tackle the renovation.

We replaced the old garage door with oak French doors. We managed to get the walls properly framed and got rid of that quirky little door. We framed the narrow window that ran the length of the roof. We insulated the place and stapled in a vapour barrier. But winter was coming, and after covering the new plywood walls with plastic we decided to wait it out.

We noticed over the winter that the insulation we'd installed had little or no effect. When spring came, we discovered that the ceiling had never been insulated, either. Once it was spray-foamed to the right height, we got to work again. We replaced the old single-pane window with a modern casement. I filled the gaps in the foundation. We brought in baseboard heaters and hired a local tradesman to hang the drywall. We put in a 220-amp circuit for Deb's kiln along with proper ventilation for it. Ceiling fans regulated the heat, and we built elaborate drywall drops to cover the array of wires the old bachelor had run willy-nilly through the garage.

Once the paint went on, the garage looked amazing. But we still had problems with the floor. The poured concrete wasn't level. The cost of pouring a whole new floor would have been huge, so we mixed cement and levelled things as best we could by hand. Once we'd sanded it smooth, we laid a layer of floor padding over a vapour barrier, then for three agonizing days knelt and pressed free-floating laminate into place. When we were finished, the place was stunning.

Nowadays, Deb's studio takes up the back end of the garage, near the new picture window. She's already fashioned some awesome art pieces she's given away as gifts. We have a second refrigerator out there, a work-out machine, weights and a warm, inviting sitting area with a TV, a stereo, a sofa, a rocker and a wing chair.

The far side of the old garage, where the quirky little door used to be, is my space. We put a loft bed there for when company comes, and I've set up an office under the bed's frame. I've got a long work shelf suspended by metal hooks, where my computer sits, and a slimmer shelf for my books and files. I face the wall when I write, but that's how I like it—the outdoors is too distracting for me. When I sit at my desk, all I can see is what's in my imagination.

A favourite picture of my wife sits right in front of my monitor. It was taken on Gabriola Island the first summer we were together. As I'm writing, I see that wonderful smiling face, and I am convinced that magic is alive in the universe. On the wall, there's a picture of the two of us standing beside a thousand-year-old cedar tree. Hanging beside that are the two eagle feathers we tied together as part of our marriage ceremony. I've also mounted a quote from the writer George Eliot: "I think I should have no other mortal wants, if I could always have plenty of music. It seems to infuse strength into my limbs and ideas into my brain. Life seems to go on without effort when I am filled with music."

My medicine box sits at the far edge of my desk. It holds the sweetgrass, cedar, sage and tobacco that we use to bless our home. There are rocks in that box, too, and gifts of tobacco I've been given for making presentations. A portable electronic keyboard, my guitar and my djembe sit beside the loft ladder. A music stand awaits the next batch of guitar music I'll try to learn.

A collection of my published titles is displayed on the narrow shelf above me, along with a photo of Deb and me on a roller coaster and an editorial cartoon of me from the *Calgary Herald* that makes our friends laugh. That shelf also holds a dictionary, a thesaurus, a manual for writing screenplays, CD copies of my radio commentaries and a stack of CDs that I'll be reviewing for my music column on the Internet. Directly above hangs a white eagle feather that belonged to the grandmother of a friend from the Sechelt Nation. I am surrounded in my writing space by the things I love and that sustain me. When I sit in that space, I feel creative and empowered.

The Creator meant for me to write. Not to think about it, not to plan for it, not to wait for inspiration, but to write to honour the gift I was given. So I come here every day and I write something. Once I've done that, I use my space in other ways: to browse the Internet, do research, play my guitar or drums, read, or listen to Brahms, or Miles Davis or the Reverend Gary Davis. Sometimes I just lean back in my chair, swivel around and gaze at the fabulous space my wife and I have built together. An art space. A space for creativity. A part of both our worlds, and a part of us joined together, for the common purpose of finding joy.

Making the Clouds Disappear

DRIVING BACK FROM Kamloops on the Paul Lake road, you rise up out of a twisting little valley onto a great stretch of tableland called Skidan Flats. It's a sagebush meadow, free range land where horses are sent to graze the summer grasses. On the north side of the road, there's always a herd of cattle, long-horned and lazy. Above the humped shapes of mountain that ring the road is the incredible azure bowl of the sky. Whether we're returning from a trip out of town or just our usual shopping and supplies jaunt, the view always astounds us.

I can't understand how people can speed through here. Deb and I tend to dawdle, and it irritates the drivers racing through at 120 clicks. But whisking through that stretch seems like cheating yourself. We always get a thrill as we top that rise. The light can dazzle you with its moods and shadings. The sky is so huge and perfect from that vantage point you feel you could be launched into it at any second.

When I was a foster kid in Kenora, Ontario, I spent a lot of time alone. The other kids in my neighbourhood had regular families, but I never knew from one week to the next whether I'd be staying or be sent off somewhere else. Other kids intuit that kind of desperation, and they steer clear of it. It didn't help that I was the only Indian kid in the neighbourhood, or that northern Ontario in the early 1960s was very small-minded. I got used to wandering around by myself, and the truth was I liked it that way.

Deep in the bush, about twenty minutes from where I lived, I discovered a table rock. It was a slab of pink granite that jutted out of moss and blueberry cover into a clearing. The rock was rutted some by the weather, but it was mostly flat, and it had a slight angle that made it easy to lie back on. With the sun pulsing down and the heat of it radiating against your back, that rock was a great place to stretch out. Nobody else knew about the rock, it seemed, and it became my own private refuge.

Lying on that table rock for hours at a time, I was introduced to the wonders of the sky. Gazing up into the heavens, I felt as though I was levitating, free of gravity. Sometimes I'd bundle moss under my head. Other times I rolled my jacket or sweater into a pillow. When you stare at the sky long enough, you come to feel that you're a part of it. As a foster kid who never fit in anywhere, I treasured that feeling.

So I surrendered myself to the sky. I'd tell myself there were pirate ships in the clouds skimming past high above, great bears or carousels or the fiery exhalations of a dragon. Sometimes, when a wispy cloud appeared, I'd hold my arms up in front of my face and blow sharply on my wrists. Then, keeping my eye on that small cloud, I'd rub my wrists together, making a counter clockwise circle. I'd concentrate, and eventually that little cloud would vanish right before my eyes. I always laughed when that happened. I felt like the world's greatest magician.

I knew it was really just the wind. I was cognizant of the everyday science all around me. But for that brief moment

I slipped free of rules and knowledge and accepted belief. I allowed myself to believe I truly had magical powers. I was often scared after I left northern Ontario for my adopted home in the south. I'd lost my table rock, but I still had the sky. Whenever things were bad or confusing or hurtful, I could always find a place to stretch out, gaze upward and feel the sky fill me. Even as I got older, that always helped me hold on.

I'm a grown man now, living in a grownup world that's short on everyday magic. There are bills to pay, chores to be done, problems to be solved. But when I take the time to wander out and find a quiet place in the sunshine, I can still make clouds disappear. I can still free myself from rules and the accepted order of things. And whenever we crest that hill and drive onto the tableland of Skidan Flats, I remember the sky's promise to me. We all have that magic within us. Look up. Look up.

Heroes

FOR A LONG time, I've been of the mind that heroes are for children. Once the world settles down around your shoulders, and *responsibility* becomes your mantra for day-by-day living, heroes get left behind. Sure, as a baseball fan I have players I admire, and as a rabid musicologist I have musicians I love listening to, but for a long time there hasn't been a distant figure who has touched my life in a meaningful way. I've just become too busy for heroes.

Life is a succession of practical tasks. Life is stubborn, plodding routine. Life is an eyes-on-the-horizon march towards success and security. There's little time for the dreaming, the idolizing and the vicarious basking in glory that heroes demand of us. Heroes are the province of childhood recollections and dinner table tales. So I was surprised when I found myself watching the 2008 Democratic presidential nomination race with great interest. Normally I'm blasé about U.S. politics. Like all Canadians, I'm inundated with American news, and I sometimes feel I know more about what's going on south of the border than I do about our own domestic situation.

But the presidential primaries caught my attention. For one, Hillary Clinton was in the race, and I desperately wanted to see a woman assume the mantle of power. Women are a lot like Indians, really. They know how it feels to be marginalized, prejudged, undervalued and over-scrutinized. So I wanted her to do well. Maybe I could score a vicarious victory from her achievements.

But I was even more interested in Barack Obama. When he secured the Democratic nomination, then squared off against Republican John McCain in their November showdown, I couldn't have been happier. If anyone understands how race affects your ability to secure a just place in society, it's a black person, and Obama's race for the White House held a lot of importance for me. I wanted him to win. I wanted to believe that there is still room in this world for someone to do the unthinkable, the unimaginable, the extraordinary, the historically outrageous.

It's not just Native people who share that wish. Women, people of mixed race, people with disabilities, the homeless, the mentally challenged, gays, lesbians, people who are under-educated and unemployed, the elderly, immigrants and youth all want to see an underdog rise up, not only to challenge the status quo but to give it a good licking. As a First Nations person who's watched and waited for an inspiring politician to rise from our ranks and lead us to equality in Canada, I saw Obama as a beacon in the darkness.

Obama's quest continued the journey begun by Abraham Lincoln. Lincoln wanted emancipation for black people. He wanted freedom and equality to be more than just poetic phrases in the U.S. Constitution. His vision was justice for everyone, and it took a war to get the ball rolling. The theme was continued later in the work of Martin Luther King, Jr. Reverend King's crusade was for the everyday rights of all people. He expressed that in a clarion call to black consciousness, but his message was for everyone. He was a pacifist who held out the possibility that salvation could come from the people themselves, if we would only heed the message. Many of us did, and things changed.

I was a boy in the 1960s. I remember the tumult of the civil rights movement. I remember the permissible racism of the white neighbourhoods where I lived—Aunt Jemima on the pancake box, the waist-coated Negro coachmen on numerous lawns, the references to Brazil nuts as "nigger toes" and black men referred to as "boys" in the colloquial conversations of men I was supposed to admire. There were "good Negroes" like Sammy Davis, Jr., Nipsy Russell and Jackie Robinson, but I recall the fear "bad Negroes" like H. Rap Brown and Stokely Carmichael evoked in my adopted white parents. Their fear was transferred onto every black person they encountered after the riots in Detroit and Watts. I remember looking at my own brown skin and wondering how that applied to me.

I couldn't frame the equation properly then, but life offered me that chance eventually. The older I got, the more aware I became of being treated as different, out of place and wrong. My white home was no shelter from that racism. My adopted parents continued to try to carve me into their own image, never thinking that the constant nicks and gouges were causing me pain.

I became a high school drop-out, a welfare case, an unemployed, homeless alcoholic and eventually a card-carrying First Nations activist. Along the way I met people of all stripes who showed me that it isn't just skin that polarizes us—it's attitude. Having labels applied to you is tiring. Fighting my way through terms like "lazy," "shiftless," "stupid," "backward" and "drunken Indian" was arduous, and the journey was seldom illuminated by models of change.

When I started to write the stories of my people as a journalist, I ran up against many historical barriers. The story of the relationship between whites and Indians was rarely told. Instead, Canadians believed what the history books told them, that grand tale about Europeans conquering the wilderness and establishing a shining nation from sea to sea to sea. They knew the names of the "explorers"—Radisson and Groseilliers, David Thompson, Alexander Mackenzie—but not those of the Indians in the canoes.

So Barack Obama's quest was my quest, too. His crusade for justice, for representation, for recognition was not just for black people but for all of us who have had to fight to be seen, heard and valued. Watching it unfold, I felt the hope Obama expressed in speeches and debates. He represented the power of one man to keep moving forward despite old hurts.

The image of Obama, arms raised in victory, showed me and marginalized people everywhere that triumph is not only possible—its time has come. We all needed that lesson, because heroes ought never to be relegated to our past. For people of all ages, heroes ought to be part of the fabric of every day.

Born to Roam

I DON'T TRAVEL very well these days. I get called out all the
time to speak at conferences, run workshops, do readings or
lecture at universities. Most of these trips are only a few days
long but, I can never wait to get home. I feel troubled by not
being able to see the lake, get out on the land or feel the quiet
all around me. Even when I'm ensconced in a nice hotel with
all the amenities, I still long for our woodstove and plank
floors. I guess I've become a homebody.

It wasn't that long ago that my life was like a sappy country song. I was always on the road again, looking at the world
through a windshield, as that old truckdriving song goes.
White-line fever raged in me, and home was always just over
the horizon. Life was about moving on.

I did a lot of hitchhiking during my late teens. There was a
gypsy feel to being young and free on the side of a road with
just a backpack and a sleeping bag. I felt like a hobo king, a
Kerouac, the kind of ramblin' boy Tom Paxton sang about. It
always seemed to be summer. I could hit the road at the drop
of a hat, and I often did. I ate at creaky truck stops and small
clapboard diners along the highway. I'd meet other kings of

the road at the hostels where I stayed; we'd share drinks and stories and a few guitar songs around a fire. Family was an ever-changing set of faces.

I was a railroad gang labourer for a while. I picked pine cones, planted trees, stoked wheat, cleaned floors, washed dishes, shovelled feed, cleaned fish and lugged construction materials in every part of Canada except the Maritimes. Every job put just enough money in my pocket for me to hit the road again.

Later, I hit the road a lot as a reporter and a documentary producer. It was the late 1980s by then. There were always issues and questions and ideas I wanted to investigate, and being on the road made that possible. The road was my university, and I majored in people. I met miners, engineers, firefighters, nurses, teachers and scientists. I sat with them in grand old homes on cultured estates and dark shacks on remote reserves. Whatever the state of their homes, most of the people I met had settled in somewhere, and I started to crave that myself.

When Debra and I first moved in together, we lived in a condo on a busy street in Burnaby. Part of me still wrestled with slippery feet. Part of me still believed there was promise just over the rise ahead. But Deb was patient and gentle, and I gradually felt more comfortable walking in through a door than out. When we moved here to the mountains, that feeling grew stronger.

I'm fifty-three now, and these old bones have grown more attached to languishing in front of the fire than to racking up the miles. I don't enjoy food much when I travel, and I can't relax enough to read. I get ornery in airports, grumbling a lot and putting on the impassive Indian face that makes Deb laugh. Only when I'm home do I feel content.

The years sneak up on you, and you're different suddenly. You realize there's no more time to be wasted. You're a
hunter-gatherer, for Pete's sake, I tell myself. You're supposed
to be out loose upon the land. You're supposed to roam, sharing stories with others around a crackling fire. But the home
fires are the only ones I care for any more. Call me an old
coot, but I've never found a five-star joint that feels as good
as home.

NORTH

WISDOM

TO BE TRULY wise is to understand that knowing and not knowing are one. Each has the power to transform. Wisdom is the culmination of teachings gleaned from the journey around the circle of life, the Medicine Wheel. Circles have no end. We are all spirit, we are all energy, and there is always more to gain. This is what my people say. When the story of our time here is completed and we return to spirit, we carry away with us all of the notes our song contains. The trick is to share all of that with those around us while we're here. We are all on the same journey, and we become more by giving away. That's the essential teaching each of us is here to learn.

Today Is a Good Day to Die

WHEN I REJOINED my people as a young man and encountered traditional and cultural teachings for the first time, my feeling of alienation vanished. Suddenly I had ways of expressing who I was, and I took them up with the enthusiasm of a starving man. But in my frenzy to become as Native as I could be, I missed out much of the intent in the teachings I was given.

For a time after I'd learned the history of the settlement of North America and the displacement of our people, I was embittered and angry. Militancy among young Native people was growing then, and I eagerly embraced it, participating in marches and protests, office occupations and sit-ins. At the high end of that energy, there were some violent confrontations and stand-offs. I believed fervently that the things we were doing were justified and right. I believed that kind of action was the answer to the forced subjugation of my people's identity, traditions and culture.

In those years, I was driven by anger. People would often tell me, "Richard, you have to have faith." That irritated me. I didn't know what I was supposed to have faith *in*, and it seemed to me that faith was a show of weakness. A man needed to act without advice or aid from anyone, I thought. So I created what I thought was a clever response. When someone told me I needed to have faith, I'd retort that the word faith was actually an acronym for Find Another Indian To Hassle.

We militants had a mantra in those days that was reputed to have come from the great Lakota Sioux war chief Crazy Horse. Everyone in what we called "the struggle" used this mantra. The words were, "This is a good day to die." We believed those words meant that, as warriors, we should be prepared to lay down our lives for the people, to fight to the end. We wore our red headbands, camouflage clothing, fringed buckskin vests and moccasins with pride, bearing that brave statement before us. Everywhere I met young Native people, that mantra was what brought us together.

One summer during that time I attended the Indian Ecumenical Conference in Morley, Alberta. A large number of traditional teachers and medicine people came there to share their teachings and ceremonies. Morley was *the* place to be seen if you were any sort of radical. Those teachings and ceremonies were what we had pledged to protect, and being there when they were practised was the ultimate proof of your worthiness.

The spirit and energy of the gathering made me uncomfortable, though. I felt wrong there—that was the only word I could find for my anxiety. As I sat in sessions and participated in rituals, I felt invalid. So, because I was not a brave person, I reacted out of my adopted militancy. Whenever I felt challenged, I simply repeated the magic words of inclusion: today is a good day to die.

One of the teachers overheard me one night. Albert Lightning was a Cree, a highly regarded ceremonialist and teacher. He approached me when there was no one else around and asked me to sit with him. Once we were comfortable, he looked at me for a long moment. "What are you so afraid of?" he asked.

He asked it directly, without an ounce of judgement in his voice. Instead, he sounded concerned and compassionate.

"I'm not afraid of anything," I said in reply.

He nodded and looked down at the ground. When he looked back up at me again, there was an earnest expression on his face. "What you said over there, those words, do you know what they mean?"

I gave him the stock militant answer, and he nodded again. "When Crazy Horse was with us," he said, "he was a great leader. He spent a great deal of time with spiritual people, and he learned the principles and values that make a leader great. He took the time to learn that the foundation of the warrior way is always spiritual."

Albert paused for a moment, then continued. "When Crazy Horse used the words 'today is a good day to die,' he did not mean that he was so brave he could give his life in battle without question. He meant that he had considered the questions. Before he took up his war lance, he spent time in meditation and prayer. He looked at the issue that might cause him to go into battle and asked himself if that issue was a worthy one. He asked himself if he was prepared to continue his spirit journey in another form over that issue.

"But most importantly, he thought about his foe, a man not unlike himself, with a family, loved ones, a tribe, a community. He thought about how the people of his foe would feel if that man were taken away on the battlefield. He prayed for their well-being, for their prosperity, for their happiness. He prayed for their future.

"If the idea of going into battle was just as strong once he had done all these things, Crazy Horse said to himself, 'If I can pray for my enemy and want those things for him that I want for myself, if I can consider him as a sacred part of Creation, like myself, then I am ready to go to battle. Today is a good day to die.'

"So when you use those words, you must know that they are spiritual words. They are not militant, angry or vengeful words. Nor are they prideful. They are the words of one who has reflected on the sanctity of life. They are the words of a truly brave person who is able to face the foe with integrity."

Albert Lightning was a very wise man. It would be years before I really got what he had told me. There was still a long time on the merry-go-round of drunkenness ahead of me. I drank because I could not defeat the foe in myself, could not shake the conviction that I was unworthy of happiness. That belief was at the core of my being, and drink washed it away momentarily. Bravery is spiritual energy, and fear is a spiritual lack. As long as I reacted out of fear, I could not face the foe with integrity. Without integrity, the battles you fight are based in ego and pride. That is the essence of what Albert Lightning told me that night.

Eventually, I found a teacher who helped me explore the dark channels of my feelings of unworthiness. She was a therapist named Lyn MacBeath. She guided me back to the days of my childhood, and together we traced the roots of my wounded psyche and spirit. She taught me that I had the strength to move beyond those primal wounds if I would allow myself to work at it. I did, and I healed. I did that work with the belief that I was born as a sacred part of everything. I did the work out of bravery, and in the process I discovered the true meaning of faith.

Ever since then, I have striven to fight any foe with integrity. Every time I am successful, I recall the words of Crazy Horse: "Today is a good day to die."

The Roller Coaster

THERE'S A PHOTOGRAPH on my desk that was taken in the fall of 2003. Every time I look at it, I smile. Snapshots capture those tiny electric moments you want to save forever.

My girl and I are in that photo. We look like excited children. Deb has her arms raised in triumph and surprise. I'm sitting beside her with a fist pumped, obviously thrilled. We were both approaching our fifties at the time, but you wouldn't know that from our faces. We were on a plummeting roller coaster, in the full pitch of that belly-dropping fall.

Deb and I had been together for six months by then. Our lives were a rollercoaster ride of discovering each other, finding each other's rhythms and feeling the world shift beneath our feet. We'd both been through a pair of marriages and a rolodex of other failed relationships. It was our emotional resumés that brought us together, actually. We both knew and appreciated the difficulties of the journey.

We didn't come together in one of the awesome emotional and sexual explosions of our younger years. Instead, we eased together in a confluence of streams. I was a First Nations man, and she was the progeny of some of the transplanted miscreants who built Australia. Her great grandmother was a

West Indian slave bought on a Fremantle pier. Both of us had struggled to find our identities, and then to express them. We had both been adopted as kids. We bore similar wounds from that and both of us had drunk too much too often. Finding each other was a breath of fresh air.

Neither of us was a very conventional person. I'd spent years on the street, behind bars and working a host of dead-end jobs. She'd worked on West Coast fishing boats, studied fused glass art with a renowned craftsman, lived in New York and partied through the hey-days of Vancouver in the early 1980s, when it was a thrilling cultural and entertainment hot spot. We both knew thieves and whores and strippers, drug dealers, bikers and madmen. We'd come to call some of them friends. We'd also rubbed elbows with financiers, celebrities, entrepreneurs, politicians and other high rollers. Somehow in that exotic mix of influences, we'd become ourselves.

The roller coaster in the picture is the old-fashioned coaster on the grounds of Vancouver's Pacific National Exhibition. It brings to mind the days of nickel candy floss, twenty-five-cent midway rides and a fifty-cent admission charge at the gate. The roller coaster's wooden frame and the small tin-can cars that shake and rattle along the track promise adventure. The romantic kind, not the gut-wrenching thrill of more modern, gravity-defying rides. Even so, it took us a few months to screw up our courage. We talked about the old roller coaster a lot, imagining how it would feel to ride it, reminiscing about the carnival rides of our youth. But whenever it came time to head to Playland and make it happen, there was always something more adult to do. We could see the roller coaster from where we lived, however, and in the evening sun it beckoned to us. Finally, one day there we were, walking up the ramp with our tickets in our hands.

The pleasure started as we waited in line. The faces of the people getting off the roller coaster were flushed with excitement. Their ride had lit up young and old alike from the inside. I was fascinated to see such joy. I shifted from foot to foot, amazed at how quickly the kid in each of us comes to the fore. Neither Deb nor I spoke as we handed over our tickets and stepped into the car. A spear of excitement pierced my belly. Deb and I were laughing, but it was that high-in-the-throat laugh of nervousness and tension. Anticipation gripped us as the roller coaster began the long, slow pull to the top. Then came the drop. Thirty metres almost straight down, then back up in a whoosh of air and energy that drew screams from us. The next plunge was even more of a rush.

We whipped around each bend and turn, giddy with uncontrollable laughter. There was none of the usual adult need to appear composed or proper. It was pure experience, and we felt totally alive.

We've been back to the roller coaster a few times since then. On each visit, I feel young and wild and dumbstruck with joy all over again. Each time, my girl and I return to our child spirits as we let go of everything that keeps us earthbound.

Staying in touch with that kid within is the secret to becoming a wise and more centred being. I wish I'd known that when I was younger. Maybe I'd have been a tad less grave, taken life's sudden turns and drop-offs less seriously. I'd definitely have had more fun if I'd allowed myself more freedom to howl with laughter and be filled with wonder. Whenever I look at that picture on my desk, I remind myself to do that from now on.

Nothing Gold Can Stay

IT WAS ROBERT FROST who wrote that "Nature's first green is gold." In that glorious eight-line poem, Frost went on to assert that "nothing gold can stay." The majority of Western critics have taken Frost to mean that anything beautiful must fade, that nothing can remain pure. When I first read the poem in the early 1970s, that's what I figured he meant, too. But our understanding of poetry, like our understanding of life, transforms with age. Standing here today, at fifty-four, I no longer think Frost's poem is about fading glories. Instead, I believe it's about triumph.

When I first encountered Robert Frost's poetry, I was living on the streets of St. Catharines, Ontario. The library was my home then, and one day I came across an old copy of *New Hampshire*, a collection of Frost's that also contained "Two Look at Two" and "Stopping by Woods on a Snowy Evening."

Something in Frost's words and phrasing caught me. *New Hampshire* was published in 1923, fifty years before I first cracked it open. Frost's world and mine were vastly different. My life then was defined by concrete, mission beds and meal tickets. But the way Frost wrote about the land called to me. I sat with his book at my favourite library carrel by the window for days. "Nothing Gold Can Stay" made me sad when I first read it. My own life seemed composed of nothing but endings, fade-outs and disappearances. Now, with Deb and I having just spent our first Christmas together as husband and wife, I see life much differently.

Our first few Christmases were celebrated with other waifs. One year we celebrated with a retired British diplomat and his wife. Another year we shared a meal with a friend whose family could not afford to get her and her boyfriend home. Deb's kids always joined us, sometimes with their dad and their great-aunt, but for the most part these affairs were patched together.

Once Deb and I moved to the lake, Christmas became a gathering with the kids. One year, we all walked up into the back country, and I toted back a fine young spruce that we decorated together. Another year, the two girls brought their beaus, and the four of them built a combination yurt/igloo in the front yard. After they left, there was always a residue of sadness. It took a few days for us, Deb especially, to get our emotional equilibrium back. This year, the kids came up a week before the big day, because their young schedules were so full. Deb and I were on our own for Christmas Day, and we made it glorious.

We rose early and exchanged our gifts. Then we loaded the car with fourteen bags stuffed with presents for the tenants of the rooming house. A good friend of ours, Doreen Willis, had spent a big part of the year filling those bags, wrapping each article individually. We also had personal gifts for the two women who live at the house and help us look after the place.

We went from door to door delivering the gifts, along with grocery coupons, cookies and other treats. We had hugs for those who could allow them, handshakes and a clap on the shoulder for the others. The smiles that broke on people's faces were heartwarming. They were touched to be remembered, included and honoured. Fourteen bags of presents. Fourteen souls. Fourteen lives.

After we left the house, we went skiing. It was a marvellous, crisp sunny day, and we skimmed down the hill with abandon, feeling like kids again. Then we drove to Jon and Irene Buckle's home to share dinner with their family. There were thirty of them, and Deb and I were soon lost in the throng of sons, daughters, in-laws, grandkids, great-grandkids and dogs.

Driving home along the pitch-dark road through ridges, valleys and gulches and then along the flats, we were tired but filled with happiness. Alone together. Seven Christmases. Seven years. Seven glories.

There are times when Deb and I envy those whose lives are built around family activities. There are times when we wonder why we are more like polite strangers than blood kin with most members of our own families. But there are also times when we can't wait for grandchildren, when we look forward to fabulous feasts with people strewn everywhere through our little mountain home.

Nothing gold can stay. Each Christmas leading up to this one shone in its own way. Those seven years aren't gone; instead, they've become the gold of our time here, our treasure, part of our stories. That's what I think Robert Frost was getting at. Riches are not defined by gold, and a brief moment can remain pure forever in the heart. Life demands that we cherish our memories, that we triumph.

Mrs. Fricke and the Bullies

IN THE SUMMER of 1966, when I was eleven, my family moved to a rented farmhouse in southwestern Ontario. Since they'd adopted me the previous May, we'd changed homes three times, and I'd never gotten a chance to really put my feet down anywhere. As I stood on that farmhouse porch for the first time, seeing the empty fields around me, I felt lost and scared and as empty as those fields.

But once we'd gotten settled, I was free to wander. There were fifty hectares on that farm in Bruce County, a mix of fallow field, hay crop, wheat and pasture. There was a wood at the back and a stream that led to a marsh, a creek and a dam a kilometre away. That land became my playground, and I spent every day out there.

I tramped the fields. I started a creature journal, in which I recorded all the animals I saw and drew pictures of them. I fished the creek and the splash pool below the dam. I watched birds. I sat in the arms of mighty trees and gazed across those wild stretches of farmland and dreamed or read or sang songs to myself. It never occurred to me to feel alone. The world was my companion, and I felt at peace.

But the thing about farms is that you never get to meet other kids. My adopted brothers were either working or uninterested in exploring, so I was left to my own devices. Although I revelled in that, by the time school rolled around I had no buddies, no peer group, no connection to any other kid. I went out to meet the bus awash in apprehension and worry.

My teacher that year was Mrs. Lorraine Fricke. She was an older woman, nearing retirement. She had grey hair, glasses and a kind smile, and she dressed in old-fashioned skirts and blouses. I'd never had a grandmother, but Mrs. Fricke fit the image I carried in my mind. That first day, she seemed to know me already. When she saw me enter her classroom, she walked right over, smiled and led me to a seat beside the window to the right of her big wooden desk.

"So you can look out at the trees," she said.

As it turned out, there was a bully in that class named Jim. His family owned the jewellery store in town. Jim was also a hockey star, which made him a big thing in that small town. Bullies always find lesser cohorts, and Jim had four other boys who supported him in his meanness. The five of them were unavoidable on the playground.

There was also a kid in my class named Dennis Edwards. Dennis was short, with big ears and a round face, and he struggled to keep up with the work. He used wacky, off-beat humour to try to wrest some acceptance from the rest of us. I found him funny, and his attempts to fit in resonated with me.

When I showed myself to be a bright student, Jim targeted me. At first it was the usual name-calling and spit-balling in class. Then it was tripping me in the hallways and bouncing balls off my head at recess. The intimidation progressed to punches on the shoulder and slaps on the back of the head. I took it all without any thought of striking back or getting revenge. I didn't want to make any waves.

But then the bullies went after Dennis Edwards. Jim took umbrage at Dennis playing hopscotch with the girls. He called

Dennis a sissy. He called him a little girl. Then he shoved Dennis, and Dennis shoved back. The rest of the pack descended on him instantly. I'd been walking in the playing field when it happened, but I saw Dennis's bleeding nose, blackening eye and tears when the bell rang.

Dennis was my only friend in class. I wanted to stand up for him. But there were five of them. I sat at my desk and listened to them bragging about the beating. When other kids joined in the laughter, I was incensed.

Sometime that afternoon, Mrs. Fricke called on me to do a problem on the board. As I stood with my back to the room, I heard the bullies grunting and talking like movie Indians. An eraser hit me in the head. I turned, picked it up and looked at it in my palm. Then I walked to Jim's desk, all the way at the back of the room, where he sat with his four friends around him. No one said a word, not even Mrs. Fricke. Everybody watched me and waited to see what I would do.

I put the eraser down on Jim's desk. He sneered at me. When he stood up, the rest of the bullies stood, too. As I took in the five of them in the silence of that room, I felt incredible heat in my cheeks and a huge knot in my belly. I was shaking, and my voice wavered when I spoke. "I'm not afraid of you" was what I said. The bullies laughed and catcalled as I walked back to my seat, but they never bothered me or Dennis again.

That day after school, Mrs. Fricke asked me to stay a minute longer. She had something for me, she said. Once all the kids had gone, she handed me a picture of Martin Luther King, Jr. He was a man of peace, she explained, and he was guided by a vision of how life could be if people were truly courageous. She said what I had done in class exemplified everything Reverend King stood for. Then she hugged me.

I read everything I could about Martin Luther King, Jr., after that, and I became an even better student. I did extra homework, helped neaten our classroom and showed Mrs. Fricke the stories and poems I was beginning to write. She brought me books to read about my people and my heritage, and we discussed them. My home life was a shambles, filled with incredible friction and pain, but in Mrs. Fricke's class I felt accepted and understood.

I got A's and B's on my first report card. On the bus on the way home, I noticed that Mrs. Fricke had written in the space for the teacher's comments, "Richard is a very honourable boy." I never forgot that. When my adopted parents read out this comment at the dinner table that night, they said she must have been referring to some other kid. I never forgot that, either.

Mrs. Fricke left school halfway through that year for health reasons, and I never saw her again. Her replacement was a disciplinarian, aloof and cold, and my marks tailed off sharply. That caused me difficulty at home. My adopted parents considered good marks a direct indicator of worth and a measure of the family itself. They revoked my privileges, including being allowed to go out on the land.

I kept the picture Mrs. Fricke had given me in one of my drawers. Whenever I felt afraid, I'd take it out and look at it, and I always found strength. Two years later, when Martin Luther King was gunned down in Memphis, I was living in a city far away from that farm. I mourned his loss, and I remembered Mrs. Fricke.

The angels in this life arrive when we need them most. They don't come in resplendent white or shining glory, but in the simple dress of an old-fashioned school teacher or the anonymous face of a stranger. In the realm of the spiritual, we are all angelic if we choose. It is, my people say, the choosing that grants us wings.

Unseen Visitors

I'VE BEEN READING a book on theoretical physics lately. It's not your usual cuddle-up-in-front-of-the-fire material, but it fascinates me. The ideas the book contains ask me to reconsider things I assumed I knew. I like that. It keeps my thoughts fresh, and it keeps me curious.

I never fared well in science classes at school. I believe it was the teaching methods that discouraged me. Dissecting frogs and making baking soda rockets and exploding volcanoes was fun but not really inventive. My reading during those years was about Ptolemy, Copernicus and Einstein's early work on special relativity. So science class was drudgery. Some part of me understood implicitly that the universe was a living, growing thing, and I wanted to understand it better. I was a long way then from the traditional teachers and awe-inspiring metaphysics of my people, but I carried that yearning like a hidden gene. Something big out there was calling for my attention.

When I did get the chance to learn about our Native beliefs, I was ready. I never had a problem accepting the presence of unseen worlds or beings. I never struggled with the concept of Great Spirit, of all things existing as energy. The strong connection between Western science and Aboriginal belief systems has become ever more apparent to me over the years. Both have the capacity to evoke wonder. It's a very human experience to peer off into a web of stars and feel awe descend on you like cosmic dust. Wonder is the place where theories are born. It's where legends and teachings and ceremonies have their genesis. Wonder connects science to philosophy. It also connects people.

There's no one among us who hasn't been floored by something unexpected, new or strange. All of us have been touched by the wondrous in something simple or common: the gleam of a dragonfly wing in the sunshine, the whirr of a hummingbird, the haunting call of a bird in the dark.

The hand drum that hangs on our wall is made of deerskin and wood. Although it's imperfect, it's beautiful in the plainness of its construction and the intent of its design. A Cree woman came to Vancouver to give a drum-making workshop when Deb and I were living there. Neither of us had made a drum before, and we were excited at the prospect.

The workshop took place at a local college. I remember it well, because of the laughter and the joy the participants took in learning something new. There were all kinds of people working together that day: First Nations, Asian, South Asian, German, Australian and English. Every face wore a look of pride.

There is a philosophy involved in drum building. From our leader, we learned that all cultural groups have drums. Drums are common to our human experience. There is also a science to the making of a drum, and I appreciated being introduced to the principles of elasticity, geometry and resonance. The day flew by. Deb and I came away with a feeling of fulfillment and a pair of great-sounding drums.

For a while, we played those drums often. Then, when a friend helped us move to our new home in the mountains, I gave him my drum as a gift. That's the tribal way. You offer things you have created, struggled for, to honour the act of gift-giving. My friend had never owned a drum, and my gift to him strengthened our friendship.

We still have the drum Deb made, and we use it regularly in ceremonies and at gatherings. That drum has been blessed and smudged. I played it during the entry song for Deb at our wedding. It's a valuable tool for us on our spiritual path. And every now and then, whether in the quiet of the evening or early morning or when the room is full of friends, that drum will make a sound all on its own. Sometimes the sound is like a pluck on the thongs that keep the drum strung tight. Other times, it's as if someone had tapped softly on its face. Sometimes the drum even shifts a little in its position on the wall.

Friends unfamiliar with drums will stare at our drum uncomprehendingly when that happens. Deb and I just smile in the drum's direction and say hello. It's as though an unseen visitor is assuring us that we are not alone, that we are being watched over and protected. That's a very special feeling, and one we welcome. Drums embody all the love and energy that went into making them, and those sounds are like that energy returning. Some people would attribute them to changes in the air, to dampness or the heat from the woodstove. But for us, the drum sounds indicate the presence of the spiritual.

Magic and mystery exist all around us. I believe that we carry moonbeams and stardust and the whirl of comet tails within, and we will merge into those elements when this physical life has ended. By greeting our universe with wonder, we prepare ourselves to receive its secrets. That's not scientific, perhaps, but it sure feels better that way.

What Needs Fixing

I GET A lot of letters and emails from people who have read my books, seen my television commentaries or heard my radio segments. It's gratifying to receive them. So often a writer is lost in those undiscovered territories from which stories, songs and poems emerge, and it's good to hear that my work is affecting folks. Most of the correspondence is congratulatory, people let me know how much they've appreciated my words and my stories. But sometimes the channel runs deeper. People write to me about the whole gamut of the Native experience in Canada, tell me how much they care about achieving equality and harmony, share their thoughts on the efforts we need to undertake to build a better country. I love to read those messages. They show me that the spiritual impetus to change neighbourhoods, communities and nations is alive and well out there.

Some of the messages I get are darker. People write to me about feeling lost, about feeling cut off from their identities, about the lack of a true cultural linchpin. They tell me how much they crave a respite from the travails of trying to "find" themselves. Some non-Native people write me to say they've found something in the spiritual ways of Native people that resonates with them. Sometimes, they feel guilty about appropriating something that's not their own.

Those letters and emails are all hard to read. They remind us of Thoreau's words: "Most men lead lives of quiet desperation and they go to the grave with the song still in them." None of us is immune to the pain of dislocation. All of us long to make peace with our identities. Perhaps the problem is not so much connecting with our cultural selves as feeling solid in the idea of ourselves as human beings, as men and women. Everybody has a song they want to sing.

My good friend Jack Kakakaway always maintained that it is our brokenness that leads us to healing. Each of us, in our own way, lives a fractured life. There would be no need for spirituality if this weren't so. By the time he was an elder, Jack had learned that the search for spirituality is the great bond that joins us. The problems of the world are not political in nature—they are spiritual. The difficulty comes when we try to solve those problems with our minds alone. Our heads can't lead us home, though; spiritual matters must be resolved with the heart. The head has no answers, and the heart has no questions, Jack would say.

Following our hearts may sound simple, but it's incredibly difficult to do. I've come to realize that living up here. Some days I do better than others. Some days, I'm able to see teachings in every leaf and rock.

It took a lot of work for Debra and me to get settled in our mountain home. We struggled with confusion and doubt, lack of skills and our initial lack of vision. Renovating this place required a large measure of faith and a bushel of desire. Neither of us is handy with tools, or even comfortable with them, but we were determined to learn.

We decided to start with the deck. The view from there was spectacular, but the stairs were wobbly, and most of the wood had rotted. We bought some home-repair manuals and studied them. We figured out how we wanted that deck to look, and then we set to work. We sawed supports, screwed them into place with our new power drill and cut lattice work to size. We managed to build a new set of stairs. We were pretty proud of ourselves when we were finished.

Next, we tackled the living room. The old bachelor who had built the house wasn't big on décor. We ripped out musty old carpet and an ugly pair of floor-to-ceiling bookcases. The walls hadn't seen paint in two decades, the ceiling fan was on its last legs, and the hanging lamp desperately needed replacement. We laid new laminate flooring, installed new patio doors, and replaced the questionable woodstove with one that met current safety standards.

We redid the kitchen the following autumn. There's a new floor in there now, too, new baseboards and fresh paint. After that, we converted the old garage into an art studio and office space. That was challenging. But I write in there now and Deb crafts fused glass. The confidence and skills we've gained will soon go into finishing the master bedroom.

Sure, some of our work looks amateurish. The paint is less than perfect in places, and the joints aren't always flush. But there's something special about shaping your own environment. I'd never experienced that before. It's not the Good Housekeeping Seal of Approval we're after. It's the good feeling of working together to create a place where our spirits can rest, where our creative energies can flourish, where peace can be found in a cozy chair.

We changed our house from the inside out. That's the only way it ever really works, and that's true for spiritual matters, too. It takes perseverance and commitment; no doubt about that. As Jack Kakakaway told me, to change you need a quality that is best expressed through an Ojibway word: yah-gotta-wanna. He was funny, that Jack. And he was right.

Feel the Breeze

AGE IS A funny thing. Some people say it's all relative, that you're only as old as you feel. Others claim we end up child-like again as the circle of years nears completion. I'm never sure which of the many aphorisms to lean on. My personal take is that aging is gravity having its way with you. As you mature, there are moments when you swear you can feel parts of you dropping.

There's a noticeable sag to the buttocks, for one thing. Somehow you've developed a portly droop to the abdomen. Where the firmness of youth once held sway, there is now only sway. Everything eventually heads south on us, and if there are jiggles accompanying our formerly insouciant saunter, we call them "fab flab" or "love handles." That's on good days. On bad days, we pinch a couple of fingers full and shake our greying heads.

It's a harder slog than it used to be getting up the timber road that leads into the mountains behind our house. When Deb and I ski, I have to stop for a rest on the longer runs. My talk is peppered with phrases like "you wouldn't believe it now, but...," "back in my prime" and "you should have seen me when..." Age and gravity are relentless yanks on our lives.

When I turned fifty-three not too long ago, we had a quiet celebration. No big party or dinner, just a calm recognition of time passing and a life fleshing out at the edges. There was no need for extravagance. Here in the mountains, days are merely days. In the relaxed plod of them, we find parts of ourselves that were lost in the frenetic pace of the city. I have become more accustomed to the soft glow of a morning fire than to the roar of traffic on a freeway. I've grown more attuned to the symphonic clarity of a sunset than to the raucous clatter of an urban street. But as I settle into my favourite chair, sometimes I find myself longing for the more elastic, more exuberant man I used to be.

My recollections are mostly about sports. Maybe it's typical guy thinking, but I can't resist the urge to measure the current me against the nimble, devil-may-care athlete I once was. When I played hockey, I was always the fastest skater on the team. Mind you, I was never more than a rec-league forward, but I loved it. Something in the power and grace of skating has always called to me.

The winter I was fourteen, I happened upon a crater the size of a swimming pool at the construction lot down the street. When the freeze came, it became my own private rink. None of the other neighbourhood kids had discovered it. I would go there at night and skate in the dim glow of distant street lights. I couldn't see very well, but I didn't need to.

I left my stick in the snow bank and flashed around that small stretch of ice in circles, figure eights and quick lateral dashes. I practised moves I'd seen in televised games, learning to turn and stop and change direction at top speed. After that, I taught myself to thread the puck between my legs, curl it on the blade of my stick and skate with it through turns and twists, dipsy-doodles and spins. I felt as though I was inventing the game for myself.

I got to be a very good, very fast skater on that construction lot, and the skill stuck with me through the years. I never mastered the other parts of the game, never scored goals by the bushel, but I could skate like the wind and make deft, accurate passes.

As often as I could, I found a team to play on. I've played on frigid outdoor rinks where chunks of the boards were missing and the area behind the nets was strung with chicken wire. I've played in modern arenas before hundreds of fans. I've played in public tournaments and in 2:00 a.m. beer leagues while a yawning attendant waited to clean the ice. On every team, it was my speed that marked me. On a lumber camp team in the 1980s, they called me Feel the Breeze Wagamese. Someone wanted to put that on the back of my jersey—they said a breeze was all you could feel when I blazed past.

My cousin Fred vanished with my hockey gear one year, and that was it for my playing days. The seven hundred dollars' worth of equipment was too much of an investment to make all over again. But I still can't look at a stretch of ice without thinking of the game. I can't watch more than a few minutes of *Hockey Night in Canada* without missing it. On cold winter nights when the sky is purple and frost curlicues at the edge of the windows, I'm still Feel the Breeze Wagamese, that jubilant kid waiting to lunge over the boards.

The particular joy of growing older is the pocket treasures you carry with you. Their power transcends the effects of gravity and time. A part of me will always be streaking forward into the fray. Living in the promise of the future, I can only look back and marvel at my incredible journey, the places I've been and the names I've carried. Feel the breeze. These days it's fair and warm.

Talking the Talk

PEOPLE OFTEN ASK ME if I can teach them to swear in Ojibway. Everyone always wants to know the cuss words. When I tell them there really aren't any swear words in Ojibway, they get all mooky-faced. How on earth can you have an entire language that doesn't let you sound off that way, they wonder. There are strong words and phrases in Ojibway, largely meant to put disrespectful people in their place, but there's nothing resembling a good old-fashioned four-letter word.

It might seem strange that Ojibway does not have its share of blistering lingo. The language is verb-based, so you could conceivably tell someone to go do any number of things. The younger generation incorporates English phrases into Ojibway to deliver messages like that. But the elders, teachers and healers speak the language in rolling, gentle tones. That generation is committed to saving the traditional talk. They have experienced firsthand the incredible changes our people have lived through. They've seen the movement away from traditional culture and towards the cities, the universities and the corporate world, and they seek to preserve the language before it disappears entirely.

Not everyone is familiar with the cultural history of Aboriginal peoples. Many folks have no idea that Native people had our languages taken away. The Ojibway I know is minimal at best. But what I do speak is vital to me, because it keeps me connected to my history and my identity. You feel a spiritual link when you speak in your original language. It's empowering and healing.

There are many reasons that our languages have faded, from residential schools to outside adoption, from political decisions imposed in the late 1870s to political choices made today. A recent study I read said that only four Aboriginal languages—Ojibway, Cree, Dene and Inuktitut—have a reasonable chance of survival. Out of the hundreds of cultures with active languages that once flourished in Canada, that's grim news.

Given this situation, it's no wonder some Native people go to extreme lengths to hide their limited ability to speak their traditional language. I once did. Because I looked so obviously Native, I was embarrassed to admit that I couldn't speak Ojibway. I felt like a fraud, a sham Indian, a less than adequate Aboriginal. So I faked it. Whenever someone asked me how to say something in my language, I came up with a creative but fictitious word or phrase.

There was theatre involved, too. Back then, Native people were expected to be stoic and guttural. So I would get all stern faced, cross my arms firmly across my chest, nod solemnly. Then I'd hold up one hand, palm out like a Hollywood Indian, and say in a deep voice, "I-owna-Honda" or "Kumbaya-Ojibway-Winnebago." I don't know if I ever fooled anyone. Mostly, people laughed. But that was the best I could do until I eventually learned some genuine Ojibway words.

I discovered when I was very small that you can rebuff hurt with humour. It was a handy tool as I grew older, too.

But the underlying shame is toxic. You come to believe that you truly are unworthy. It can take a long time to heal yourself from that.

Learning the traditional talk brought me forward. When I spoke my first word in my language, I felt reborn. That's not an overstatement. The word rolled off my tongue, expanded into the air around me, and I was Ojibway. Instead of a shy, scared, adopted kid using theatrics, I was a First Nations man. I'm still far from fluent. Sometimes I go months without uttering an Ojibway word out loud. But the prayer I say at the shore of the lake every morning is always an Anishinabek offering.

When your language disappears, so does your ability to greet the world in a traditional manner. That's a huge thing to lose. I was created to be a male, Ojibway human being. Speaking my language allows me to reaffirm that.

When you lose your original language, your identity is altered. You feel clumsy walking around in your own skin. That's true not just for Indians but for immigrants, anyone who has sought another shore in pursuit of a dream. Society asks everyone who's been displaced to surrender parts of themselves in order to be accepted, and language is often the first thing to go. Reclaiming your language is like coming home. You don't need cuss words to express that.

Wasting It

ONE EVENING LAST summer, I stood out on our deck with a group of friends. We had gathered to enjoy some great barbecue, the quiet of our mountain setting and the sublime enjoyment of watching night settle over us. The sky that evening was awesome. It seemed to be full of stars and the incredible variation of light that spoke of planets, nebulae and galaxies.

We stood there looking up, and none of us had words. The night sky is like that. It silences you with the magnitude of its mystery. Ojibway people have legends of the Star People who came once long ago to deliver the teachings, stories and ceremony meant to direct our lives. For a long while now, looking up at the sky has given me heart. So we stood in rapt silence, and then someone pointed to a speck of light moving eastward across the heavens.

It was the space station. As we watched it sail across the sky, I pondered how far we've come as a species. To see evidence of the human mind's potential looping around the planet was sublime. To think of that vehicle being launched into the sky to increase our understanding of the universe was wonderful.

Once the space station was gone, the night became a time for friendship, for conversation. There are entire universes in each of us, and learning about them is endlessly fascinating. As Deb and I watched the last tail lights blink out of sight and the dark reclaim its dominance, I felt grateful that there will always be new and unfamiliar territories to explore.

When I heard about a Canadian billionaire spending $35 million to become a tourist on the space station, it struck me as outrageous. Here was a man with riches galore, and all he could think to do with it was take a ride. Here on earth, $35 million would change a lot of things. You could fill a lot of hungry bellies. You could put a roof over many people's heads. You could send deserving kids to university. You could bring water to parched countries. You could help create renewable energy.

Instead, when Guy Laliberté's ride was over, he landed on a planet where nothing had changed. The opportunities his money held had vanished. From space, the earth looks placid; it's only on the ground that you can see the turmoil we live in. From space, we are a shining blue marvel. On the ground, we are growing more and more desperate as time passes. But he had fun, and I guess that's all he thought about.

There are sufficient resources right here, right now, to change things. There always have been. That's been Creator's vision all along. There's enough raw material, creativity and money to keep our world safe, productive and nurturing. Billionaires in space change nothing. Wealth comes from other people, and there's a moral obligation to repay them.

We've allowed the media to fashion our images of success. Some years ago, I watched aghast as Ryan and Trista's wedding went prime time on a major U.S. network. They were regular people who had been made famous by reality television. When they married, the expense was horrendous—estimated at $3.77 million. Later, Oprah gushed as Trista told her about the half-million dollars she'd spent importing thirty thousand roses. Neither of them seemed to consider the effect that amount of money, if put to earnest work, could have had on the world at large.

There are those who might say. "Let them have their special day," or "That amount wouldn't really change anything." Those people need to know about Babs.

Babs was a chronic crack addict. She worked as a street prostitute to support her habit. She got old and broken down, and when Deb and I met her she was looking for a room, somewhere she could find sobriety and a new beginning. Once she'd settled into the rooming house and got some months of drug-free living under her belt, we hired her to do the cleaning there.

One day, Deb asked Babs, "If you had one dream that could come true for you, what would it be?" Without hesitation, Babs said that she'd always dreamed of going to Africa to work with starving children. She'd had that dream a long time, but she didn't know how to get started on making it real. All but a few of her teeth had rotted away as a result of her drug use, making it hard for her even to go to a job interview. She carried a lot of shame and hurt, and she was too embarrassed to smile in public.

We thought that dream was incredible for a person who had been down for such a long time. Babs impressed us with her honesty, and we wanted to find a way to help her. Neither of us had the money to pay for huge dental bills, and the agencies we spoke to had no measures to get those costs covered. Then one day, sitting in our dentist's chair, Deb mentioned Babs and her dream.

"I guess we'll have to get her smile back then, won't we?" That's what our dentist said. He offered his services, and we approached the agencies again. But none of them could cover the costs even with a dentist on board.

When we got married, Babs was there to help us celebrate. She looked awesome in a mauve sun dress and heels. We'd asked people to give us a donation for Babs' dental work in lieu of a wedding gift, and by the end of the day we had collected $645.

Two days later, our dentist called. He said he could cover everything but the lab costs for dentures, $680. If we could come up with that amount, he said, he could start the work immediately. Deb and I were ecstatic. We paid the lab costs with the donated money, covering the balance out of our own pockets, and a week later Babs was in the chair. Two weeks after that, she greeted us in the hallway of the rooming house. She flashed a beaming, wonderful smile for the first time in decades.

What's all that got to do with billionaires in space? Everything. Exorbitant spending hurts. When Canada and British Columbia shelled out billions for the Winter Olympics, nothing changed. After sixteen days of vainglorious hosting, the world was still in the same condition. The potential in those billions of dollars disappeared. There is enough for everyone on this earth. There always was. When you gaze up at the sky on a starry night, that's what we need to remember.

Healing the Spirit

HEARING OF A suicide calls forth only silence at first. There's nothing you can say. Language vanishes into the void as the heavy punctuation of a life ended prematurely settles on your shoulders. A halt, a full sentence stop. An emptiness invades your spirit, and you understand clearly the nature of powerlessness.

Indians die at rates five to six times higher than the rest of the population. Among our youth, that translates to mean an incredibly high incidence of suicide. Our mortality rates at birth and from disease, violence and suicide have always been far greater than the norm. In the nation state at large, the prevalence of suicide among First Nations youth is a more pressing issue than any land claim, treaty negotiation or rights dilemma. It's far more important than payments aimed at allaying old hurts, and far more vital to our well-being. Native people don't need to die in such numbers. We need to live. But for many of us, life brings such soul-eroding despair that it's an arduous journey to continue.

I learned something of this as a kid. When I was adopted by a non-Native family and plucked from my northern life, I confronted swift and incomprehensible change. There were no words to adequately frame what I felt. Pain existed at a non-verbal level. But fortunately for me, there was baseball.

In my northern schoolyard when I was nine, there was no room for a ball field. There was barely room in all that bush and rock for a playground at all. Our games were kickball, tag or hide and seek. So the game my new classmates played at recess and during lunch hour was a mystery to me. When I was picked to play right field one day, I had no idea what to do. I'd never thrown anything as round and perfect as a softball, and my first throw from the outfield missed badly. When I took my first swing at a pitch, I spun around completely and fell on my face. Everyone laughed, even the teacher. I walked back into the school building with my head hung low. In my gut I felt four things: fear, anger, embarrassment and shame.

I feared I would never fit in or be accepted. I was angry at the laughter, embarrassed at my inability to do what others took for granted and ashamed that I had failed. I couldn't raise my head in class for fear of the smirking looks that would come my way. No kid wants to let on that they feel like a dumb outsider.

No one knew the depth of the feelings my encounter with a strange game had engendered in me. But I was inventive and courageous, and I made up my mind to learn what the game was all about. I signed books on baseball out of the library and I studied them every night. In a book called *Baseball in Words and Pictures*, there was a formula I could follow. From then on, I was determined to implement the science of the game.

In the pasture beside our house stood a crumbling old sheep barn. On the barn wall, I painted the dimensions of a strike zone, and from here I measured out the eighteen metres to the pitcher's rubber, which I marked with a scrap of old board. Every day from then on, I threw an India rubber ball at that barn and retrieved the grounders with a borrowed glove. I practised until I could hit the strike zone every time and scoop grounders effortlessly. After that, I started throwing the ball as high up on the barn's wall as I could. When it sailed back in a long looping arc, I would chase it and try to catch it. I spent a lot of time hunting it down in the long grass at first, but eventually I could gauge the flight of the ball through the air and snag it with my glove.

Next I took a bat into the pasture, tossing the ball up and trying to hit it. The book had said to keep my swing level, to start with my hips and let my hands follow them through to make contact with the ball. At first I failed miserably. No matter how hard I tried, I could not hit that ball. But after a few days, I was arcing the ball high out into the field. I'd sprinted after it and hit it back the other way. I practised alone. Although I did it out of those hard feelings in my gut, I not only learned the skills, I came to love the game.

Every night as I fell asleep, I imagined myself as a hero on the ball diamond, racing around the bases to the cheers of my teammates. But I was still too shy to try out what I was learning, so I paced around the fringe of the diamond at school while the other kids played. Then a challenge came from another school, and the rules were that everyone from each class had to play. Grumbling, the boys in my class stuck me out in deep right field, where I could do as little damage as possible. Well, I made several great catches in the outfield that day, and I hit the home run that won it for my team. My throws were hard and on the money. I started to be the first one picked in every game after that, and the feelings in my gut vanished like a puff of chalk on the baseline.

What does this have to do with suicide? Everything.

Every Native person, young or old, who confronts a system that mainstream people take for granted carries those same four feelings: fear, anger, embarrassment and shame. Left unattended, those feelings can corrode your spirit. In a very real sense, that is the nature of Native life in Canada—dealing with the lethal stew of emotions that come from a marginalized life. All of us, reserve-based or urban, have confrontations with established systems that confound us, and we have the same simmering reaction. Some of us learn to navigate the territory. Others don't. Either way, the challenges are great.

There's a part of me in every Native kid who chooses the dark way out. Somewhere deep inside I'm still that frightened, lonely youngster who desperately wanted to make sense of things. There's something in that all of us can relate to, actually, but we get so busy and so insular with our manufactured lives that we forget we are part of the same human family. Nonetheless, every needless death lessens us and diminishes our light.

Suicide hurts everyone. For Native people in Canada, it's an epidemic. On some reserves, the rate of youth suicide is horrendous, and there's incredible agony for those left behind. The only cure is prevention, and when First Nations leaders discuss the future of our people and chart an agenda for change they'd better start with the issues concerning our youth because this is the generation we will eventually hand the future to. We need our youth strong. We need them here.

Truth and Reconciliation

THE REALITY OF Native life in this country is not expressed by our politicians. It's not articulated by radicals or militants. Neither have our elders, teachers and healers adequately captured it, though they have come closest. Instead, the most significant expression lies in the voices of our youth. The majority of our population is younger than thirty, and these young people have suffered because of our failed efforts and our unhealed pain.

Canada took an important step along the healing path in 2008. The members of the Truth and Reconciliation Commission have a mandate to cross the country and listen to the stories of Indian residential-school survivors. Through the courage of survivors to lift the veil of secrecy, all Canadians will learn something of the pain and heartbreak that is the legacy of those schools. Those stories will be compelling and they will lead to healing. But the commissioners and the country need to heed the clamouring of our youth, too. The burden of our collective future is on their shoulders.

I was in Saskatoon recently for the Anskohk Aboriginal Literary Festival, a celebration of artistic expression. Native people in Canada have not disappeared. We have become creators of note, and that festival was an inspiring and entertaining place to be. The third night was devoted to an open mic stage for emerging Native writers. As an established author, it was my honour to watch those young people perform.

One by one they took the stage, and one by one they exploited misconceptions about Aboriginal realities today. They rapped, for the most part. They drew on the argot and poetries of the black American experience to cuss, detail and shout out the incredible baggage of hurt they carry. Their words and rhythms left no doubt about what their lives are like.

They rapped about suicides of those far too young to die. They dissed a world in which young girls are duped into prostitution. They rhymed about the angst of homes rocked by violence, neglect, addiction and abuse. They expressed the anger and resentment of young people tired of the alcohol, drugs and gang culture that have usurped the ceremony, ritual, language and philosophy they ought to be able to claim as their own. They raged about displacement. They unloaded blame at the adults who have forsaken tribal teachings for materialism. They seethed and they hurt and they let it go, and I was proud of them. Some say our tribalism can't find voice in another form of music that's not our own, but the room that night was filled with electronic drum heartbeats and honour songs rapped in vitriolic honesty. It was an awesome spectacle.

We owe these kids more. We owe them our truths. We owe them our apologies. We owe them a commitment to our own healing, however hard and bleak the journey may be. We owe it to them to become an empowered people who have learned the importance of forgiveness. Truth and reconciliation are not, as former Assembly of First Nations leader Phil Fontaine so righteously proclaimed, "all about the survivors."

They are about the descendents of those survivors, too. The brunt of the residential school experience is being borne by the younger generation. That's the straight truth, and it needs to be acknowledged. For every dollar paid out to the original survivors, an equal amount should go to initiatives geared towards empowering our kids: education, employment, healing. That's how we'll achieve real reconciliation.

People who have been hurt often go on to hurt others, and our unhealed pain as Native people has deeply affected the lives of our children. If we want self-government, we must accept that we are responsible for governing the development of this young generation, for nurturing them and aiding them towards the fullest possible expression of themselves. The words of our young writers shouldn't be penned in isolation and loneliness. They should be heard in a circle of those who share the pain and yearn for the same peace. We seek truth and reconciliation to build a better country for those who follow. If that isn't our aim, all our efforts will be for naught.

Surviving the Scoop

OUR CABIN IS nestled in the mountains. At least, that's how it feels. Living so close to the land, we hear stories in the whisper of the wind through the pines, tales in the patter of rain, legends in the snowfall that comes with the first sharp slice of winter. Mushrooms, ferns and open surges of granite become connections to a larger spirit. Wise and ancient voices reside in the most common of things.

Safe in the lap of all these stories, I marvel at how easily this was once taken away from me.

Debra and I were in Winnipeg recently. We'd been invited to a conference that dealt with survivors of the Sixties Scoop. Back in the 1960s, the Canadian government actively promoted a program that scooped Native kids from their homes. Many were adopted into non-Native families who lived hundreds or thousands of miles away, in Louisiana, Florida, Texas or distant cities and towns across Canada. There's not much space devoted to this in our history books, but it's a part of Canada's history nonetheless.

The once-closed files of those adoption agencies are open now. People displaced as kids can ask for their records to find out where they originated. Of all the possible questions that uprooted generation has, the biggest one, and the most painful, may be why we were forcibly cut off from our roots. For the great majority of us, the homes we landed in saw no need to let us know where we came from. "Adopted," in the parlance of the day, meant "no longer Indian." Thousands of us were denied the fundamental right to know who we were created to be.

This sad chapter in our country's history followed closely on the heels of the closure of the residential schools. To those affected, the Scoop felt like a continuation of the same genocidal policy. For me, it meant the door was effectively slammed shut on my identity. I stood stark and alone as a fencepost in a field of snow. That's how it felt to me.

The conference I was invited to drew many people who share that legacy. It also drew a professional circle of people who deal with our demographic; social workers, teachers, government ministry workers and policy developers. We gathered in a place called Thunderbird House, named for those spiritual beings that bring messages from Creator. We opened in the ceremonial way most of us had had to fight to rediscover and reclaim. The prayer, the song and the reverberations of the drum felt like a homecoming.

It was my task to present the opening address, and I couldn't sleep the night before. I tossed and turned and worried. There were a hundred avenues I could take in approaching the issue. As I looked back over my life and saw again the profound impact of the decision to remove me from my people, I was torn about how to express what that meant. There had been moments when the pain and the confusion were so intense I felt as though my skin was peeling off. There were beatings and martial discipline that scarred me. There was abandonment and neglect. There was a feeling of melancholy that I carried for years, a haunting I was at odds to explain. Even when I found my people again, there were feelings of inadequacy, cultural embarrassment, anger and fear to overcome. So it was hard to decide what I should say.

I ended up talking about baseball. I talked about encountering a game that was foreign to me but that every other kid took for granted. I spoke about what I felt in my belly as the laughter of my classmates rolled over me. Shame at not being able to do what they did so easily. Anger at being mocked and belittled. Fear that I might never measure up in this strange new world. Resentment that no one had let me know things would be so different. I described for the people at the conference how those bitter feelings ate at me. Loneliness can be such an onerous weight. But then I spoke about gritting my teeth and learning the game and ending the laughter of the others at the same time as I eased those feelings in my belly. I talked about the courage it takes to confront a foreign system, to inhabit it and make it your own. I shared how freeing that is, how healing.

I closed my talk with baseball's central metaphor: all of us working together can help each other make it home. That's what it's really all about in the end for everyone, not just Indians. Taking away someone's right to know who they are is a sin. But it's also a sin when there's no one around to help you. It's incumbent on everyone who has ever felt the lash of displacement to be on the field when the new kid shows up with no idea how to play the game.

Now that those adoption files are open, there are going to be a lot of people in that position. They'll walk into our pow-wows, our ceremonies and our events with no idea of how to present themselves. They'll have no idea how to wear their skin. We need to be there when they show up. We need to extend a hand in welcome and make them feel at home.

When you survive something titanic, it makes you stronger. It can make you wise and gentle if you've learned the lessons well. In the end, you're not a survivor anymore. You've become who you were created to be.

Dog-Wise

I'VE READ A lot of metaphysical books over the years. When I was a teenager hanging out in libraries, I discovered shelves of books about achieving your greatest potential. I read *Born to Win*, all the transactional analysis books, Carlos Castaneda on the teachings of Don Juan. Kahlil Gibran was big back then, and so was R.D. Laing, whose book *Knots* tied me into a great psychiatric knot of my own. It was all hip and cool, fodder for a young mind searching for answers.

I augmented those books with readings from the works of Freud and Carl Jung. I dipped into Nietzsche, *The Art of War, The Tibetan Book of the Dead, Zen and the Art of Motorcycle Maintenance*. I spent one memorable rainy weekend with the Upanishads. My head swam with ideas, and while I was struggling to find work or even a predictable routine for my days, those books kept my spirits up and my intellect on fire.

In the 1980s, I discovered Edward de Bono's Course in Thinking, books on dysfunctional families and co-dependency by John Bradshaw and Melody Beattie, M. Scott Peck's *The Road Less Traveled*. If you were looking for answers, it seemed there was a host of writers, talkers, celebrities and gurus, all with the definitive solution.

Pop psychology was big business, and there was a huge audience and readership for it. Self-help was the buzz word, and I was right in there helping myself. I wore Birkenstocks. I bought crystals, incense, candles, relaxation tapes, mindfulness meditation CDs, recordings of shimmering instrumental music and a hundred varieties of tea. Along with all of that, I had my First Nations sacred medicines, smudging bowls, eagle feathers, hand drum and rattles. I visited psychics, seers, shamans, medicine people, channellers and people who communed with spirits from vanished civilizations. I went to seminars, workshops, lectures, experiential gatherings, sharing circles, warrior weekends and self-parenting retreats. I was prayed for, prayed over and preyed upon. If there were solutions to the problems in my life, I was hell bent on finding them.

All that searching took a lot of energy. Everywhere I went there were posters and brochures advertising the next big thing, the next breakthrough that would lead me to bliss. Mayan priests, Aztec shamans, Toltec teachers and even a reincarnated spirit from the land of Mu offered to bring me back to the teachings. It was mind-boggling. For a while there I didn't know whether I should bang a gong, beat a drum, play a flute, tinkle a bell or stand on my head in a corner.

Nowadays, I've realized that all I need to know about successful living and psychic health I can learn from my dog. Molly doesn't charge exorbitantly by the hour. She doesn't use ethereal language. She can communicate effectively using just her eyes, and there's a spirit in her that's kinetic and magical. If ever there was a being blessed with awareness, it's Molly.

Molly is wise. She's sage. She lives entirely in the moment, and she finds joy in everything. She eats regularly, takes a substantial nap every afternoon, drinks a lot of water, stretches before doing anything and is never afraid to express love or to ask for what she needs. She's never too busy to listen, never too overwhelmed to find the smallest thing interesting and never pretends to be anything other than what she is. She welcomes everyone with abandon and feels sad when they leave. No one is neglected when it comes to Molly sharing her enthusiasm, and she's willing to be friends unless you give her a reason to be skeptical. Molly knows there's nothing better than feeling the sun on your belly and nowhere as comforting as home.

Life is much simpler now that I've become dog-wise. There are no thick books to read, no products to buy, no deep meaning to search for. Instead, there's the satisfaction of knowing that the world is full of interesting smells and sounds and sights, of wonder and infinite possibility, and that if you venture out into it, you'll always find someone willing to take a walk with you.

Wolf Tracks

THERE WERE WOLF tracks on the gravel road this morning. They ran along the roadside for a good quarter of a mile. If you weren't paying attention, you could easily mistake them for the paw prints of a large dog. They were at least a hand span across, and the animal's weight had pushed the prints deep into the muck. They veered off suddenly up a steep incline, as though the wolf had sensed something and decided to vanish. Small packs of coyotes dwell in the ridges behind our home. We've seen and heard them many times. Now and then they'll ramble around eating the dog or cat food left out on people's decks. But wolves are oddities here. I can recall seeing them once, out on the lake ice in the dead of winter. So the tracks surprised and enthralled me.

As I contemplated the wolf's presence, ideas and shards of knowledge whirled through my head. I've never been close to a real wolf, but I was raised with the same mythology about the animal as everybody else. Wolves are creatures of mystery. They are beasties of the full moon, with long shadows. They are spectres, phantoms, shape shifters, amber-eyed denizens in the realm of our darkest fears. They are remnants of our primordial past, prowling the perimeters of memory: lank, lean and patient as hell.

I was twenty-four when I rejoined my people. Whenever my family took me out on the land, a keen thrill ran through me. As foreign as the bush was to me, I seemed to be connected to it. I was excited by the depth of the shadows among the trees, by the light splayed on a table of granite by the shore, by the smell of bog and marsh wafting across a bay. The land felt alive. When I was out there standing on it, I felt alive, too, fully alive for perhaps the first time in my life.

I felt that kinetic jolt of connection when we first moved here, and I experience it every morning when I walk. It's not just the necessary task of walking the dog that calls me out; it's the land itself, the lingering feel of wild. I thought I'd never lose that sense of being joined when I first discovered it, but I learned it can be easily forgotten. I can seal myself off from that spiritual calm, that joyful feeling of belonging, with the simple act of closing a door. That bothers me. As a Native person whose ceremonial and spiritual sense stems from a relationship with the land, I don't feel comfortable knowing I can shut that off like a light switch. As a human being with stewardship obligations to the planet, this embarrasses me. As a writer who often expresses themes of kinship, I'm stunned by the realization.

The easy way out is to say that we all have to work to survive, and my job involves being indoors at the computer. Moreover, I could add, the world demands a certain distance from us; we can't be meditative and earth-conscious all the time. We can't experience a primordial thrill with each breath. But that's what we should strive for, I believe, that charge in the belly that says we are not alone and the world is not ours to order. The planet is not here for us. Rather, we are here for the planet. Something as simple yet confounding as a wolf track can take us back to that.

From the Ground

I'VE BECOME A frequent flyer. From Kamloops it's possible to connect to anywhere, and over the past few years it sometimes seems as though I live in airports. Nodding off in economy class and waking up on the airport runway of a far-off city is as common for many people as easing into our driveways. But for me, it's still a strange event.

When I was a young man, my idea of the country came from long days spent hitchhiking. I crossed Canada numerous times that way. The memories of my late teens and early twenties are marked by the charcoal ribbon of a highway stretching westward in the glint of a setting sun. I always had a book with me, and my memories are tied to that too. Waiting for a ride on the sweep of curve that leads past Portage La Prairie on a windy day in May is all dust and noise from tractor trailers and the words of William Faulkner.

As a free spirit then, I stopped and worked wherever I could, usually staying only as long as it took me to get paid. I've been a tree planter, a ditch digger, a sugar-beet picker, a farm hand, a railroad-crew labourer, a dish washer, a fish cleaner, a marina helper and a big-rig washer. It seems sometimes that I worked in every whistle stop west of Thunder

Bay. I met other itinerant workers on the road, in hostels, in rundown bars where the draft beer was a dime and on street corners where we waited for trucks to stop and pick up the crew needed for that day. Talk was all we had to fill those idle hours, and I heard a lot of stories about a lot of places. When the work was through, it was back on the road for me, always heading west, always bearing the hope that the next town, the next city would reveal itself to be the refuge I was seeking. There were romantic moments when the song of the open road filled me, but most of the time I just wanted to get going. In those days, it was the moving itself that defined me, and I knew nothing else.

Recently, I had the chance to drive those same highways. From nine thousand metres, the country is a mere patchwork of territories. You get a sense of its size and scope through an airplane's porthole windows, but the feel of the country and of the people who live here is missing. Driving from Kenora, Ontario, back to Kelowna allowed me to see things again from the ground up.

Our trip took us from the jut of the Canadian Shield across the Prairies, through the undulation of the foothills and on into the enormous push of cordillera in the B.C. Interior. I experienced a sense of timelessness in the mist of early morning in rustic Whitewood, Saskatchewan. There's still a pioneer spirit in Moose Jaw, Swift Current, Gull Lake and Maple Creek. In the cow country of Alberta, you can feel the lingering presence of the buffalo. Gazing eastward as the sun sets in the foothills, you can't help but be moved.

Canada from the ground is awesome. People everywhere are doing their thing, making the country work: truckers, wheat farmers, ranchers, hoteliers, work crews. The staunchness of spirit displayed by a truck-stop waitress can be captivating: efficiency and a down-home-folks attitude all at once. In small-town convenience stores, there's time to chat up the owner and get the low down on the cost of things these days, politics, the younger generation. When you strike up a conversation with the other travellers pulled over at a spectacular viewing spot, you hear about life in Fond du Lac and Dunnville and Shubenacadie. Beneath it all is the land, breathing, pulsing, continuing to define us.

Certainly there are problems and tough political issues to be faced. My people still suffer the brunt of government indifference. Canadians in general feel the sharp economic pinch and the effects of climate change. Prices soar, disease threatens, and we have yet to find a political party that can generate sufficient enthusiasm about its policies to form a majority in the House. But despite all that, I think we live in the greatest country on earth. There's potential for social greatness here. Whether we are Ojibway, Greek, Scottish, English, French or Turkish, this country offers us hope. You need to get out there and look at the country from the ground to really see all that.

My frequent-flying experience will be different from now on. Gazing out the window as the land passes beneath me, I'll remember the feel of the land, the pitch and sway of voices, the timbre of the story. It's a wonderful tale. To be continued.

Photo by Debra Powell

RICHARD WAGAMESE (1955–2017), an Ojibway from the Wabaseemoong First Nation in northwestern Ontario, was recognized as one of Canada's foremost First Nations authors and storytellers. He authored fifteen books including his bestselling memoirs *One Native Life* (2008) and *One Story, One Song* (2011), which received the George Ryga Award for Social Awareness in Literature. His acclaimed novel *Indian Horse* (2012) was the 2013 People's Choice winner in CBC's Canada Reads competition. His final book, *Embers* (2016), a collection of Ojibway meditations, was shortlisted for a BC Book Prize.